Business in Action

'The Business of Business'

Andrew Gillespie

Hodder & Stoughton

A MEMBER OF THE HODDER HEADLINE GROUP

Orders: please contact Bookpoint Ltd, 130 Milton Park, Abingdon, Oxon OX14 4SB. Telephone: (44) 01235 827720. Fax: (44) 01235 400454. Lines are open from 9.00 - 6.00, Monday to Saturday, with a 24 hour message answering service.

British Library Cataloguing in Publication Data
A catalogue record for this title is available from the British Library

ISBN 0 340 84820 0

First Published 2002

Impression number   10 9 8 7 6 5 4 3 2 1
Year   2007 2006 2005 2004 2003 2002

Typeset by Transet Limited, Coventry, England
Printed in Great Britain for Hodder & Stoughton Educational, a division of Hodder Headline Plc, 338 Euston Road, London NW1 3BH by Bath Press Limited, Bath, England

How to use this book: advice for students of business

This book focuses on the various aspects of organisations that determine their performance. Each chapter considers a particular area of business such as market research or the economic environment and mixes business theory with real life examples. The many business stories that run throughout the book highlight business in action (hence the title!), hopefully bringing the study of the subject alive. The stories also serve to demonstrate the integrated and synoptic nature of the subject- success or failure is rarely the result of one thing; it is a combination of factors and decisions that create the right or wrong circumstances. Reading "Business in Action" should therefore encourage students of business to think broadly and understand the importance of interrelationships within a business and with the external environment. You can either read the book from start to finish (and naturally we hope you do!) or dip into particular sections as you wish. At the end of each chapter there is a question to help you to reflect on the material that has been covered. The questions usually provide a particular context and ask you to think of the key factors or the main issues that would determine a firm's actions in this situation. Success in the study of business usually requires the ability to think critically- to distinguish the important from the trivial, the most significant factors or the main problems facing you. So rather than just coming up with a list of ideas, try to produce a supported argument and spend time deciding which of the many possible factors are most relevant. If you are working in groups you can compare your list with those of others and discuss the relative strength of your arguments. These activities should help develop the skill of evaluation (weighing up arguments, considering the relative merits of different issues) that is absolutely essential for success in business studies as well as building an awareness of the breadth of factors that need to be considered for many decisions. Completing these questions should therefore develop the critical skills needed in many case study based examinations and throughout business studies. Suggested answers to the end of chapter questions are provided where relevant but these are merely ideas to help you if you need it. The main thing is for you to weigh up the various factors involved in a decision and decide on the most critical.

We hope you enjoy reading Business in Action and that it adds to your understanding of the subject. Remember Business Studies keeps evolving and relevant stories appear in the news everyday; so keep reading, listening and watching to build up your knowledge and enrich your understanding even further.

Contents

Introduction

Business is all about taking inputs, doing something with them and producing an output that consumers want. Take people, machines, materials, money and a bit of good old entrepreneurship, mix them up, and what comes out is a series of products and services that people will want. Repeat the recipe a few times, and a few years later you're a millionaire.

If only it was as simple as that. In reality you have to work out what it is you are going to offer that customers will be prepared to pay for; you have to work out how you are actually going to produce it and how to make sure that the final result is worth more than the value of the inputs you have used up. And that's just the start. Even when you know what you are doing, you have to organise everything, keep control of what is happening, make sure that the customer is happy, keep an eye out for new things coming on the market, make sure that the other people working for you are happy, fight off the competition, and so on. And if you are lucky, somewhere along the line you might get a profit for all your hard work – but don't count on it!

Business is difficult – whether you are a big or a small organisation, you are faced with customers who are likely to change their minds or want something different in the near future. Competitors will try to take away any advantage you might have over them, or enter your markets just when you think you are safe. Suppliers will want more for less, and employees wanting to further their career will expect you to help them do it. And then the government is almost bound to put all sorts of regulations in your way, so that you have more forms to fill in than you know what to do with. To cap it all, there's probably a group of outside investors who cannot understand why you cannot make them more money more quickly. It makes you wonder why anyone starts up a business at all.

Of course being in business, whether it's your own company or working for someone else, can be challenging, and if you get it right it can be satisfying both in terms of having achieved something for yourself and in terms of monetary rewards. If your business grows, you may have created something to be proud of. As well as making yourself money, you have probably helped to employ other people and created products and services that might not have been there otherwise; you might even have put something back into society! More than that, you have faced a challenge and won through.

This book is about the trials and tribulations of business – the theory and the reality. It aims to show you what business is supposed to be about, and to consider some of the most fascinating business stories and events in recent years, for example: Virgin Airlines taking on British Airways, Napster threatening the whole basis of the music industry, the stumbling progress of the old giants such as BT, the rise and painful fall of the dot.coms, the focus and consistency of McDonald's, the value-adding humour of SouthWest Airlines, and the ground-breaking activities of firms such as Dell.

This book should be a valuable read for anyone wanting to learn about, think about and even fall in love with business. It does not aim to be a textbook in the traditional sense, but to do much more than that – it aims to make you passionate about business and eager to learn and study more. Remember: business has the power to change lives, to make or break people, to create corporate heroes and villains. Now read on.

Business forms and stages of growth

What is business?

A business is something created to make a product, a good or service. It is an organisation made up of people who get together in some way to achieve their objectives. They organise themselves to fulfil their goals, often to gain a profit. But profit is not the only goal a business can have; a business may be created to cure patients (hospital), to look after inmates (prison), or to reduce poverty (charity). In fact, any group of people focused on producing a good or service to offer to customers can rightly be called a business.

What do businesses do?

The underlying activities in any business organisation can be categorised as:
- marketing – identifying customer needs, determining what needs to be produced, pricing it, promoting it and distributing it
- operations – producing the actual good or service required
- purchasing – buying in resources; controlling stock levels
- human resource management – managing the people within the organisation
- finance – managing the money: raising it, distributing it and collecting it
- innovation – developing new products and services for the customer.

Of course, these activities may differ in importance from one organisation to another; in the service sector, for example, stock control is less significant than in manufacturing. Also, the way the activities are carried out will vary. A sole trader will carry out all of them alone (or buy in expertise), while a multinational company is likely to have specialist departments for all these different functions. But ultimately all businesses must know their customers, produce a product, manage the money and utilise their people effectively whatever their scale and nature.

For business success, these various elements must be effectively integrated – there is no point in promoting something which you cannot produce, or planning for a scale of production you cannot afford to establish.

Success in business is therefore about managing resources effectively. This means working within constraints – deciding how to use and combine the available resources most effectively.

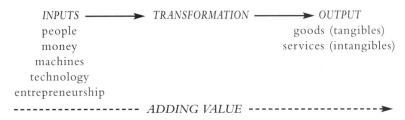

Business as a transformation process

Whatever type of organisation we look at, be it a university or a publisher or a dot.com company, it involves a transformation process. Organisations take inputs and transform them in some way to achieve outputs.

$$INPUTS \longrightarrow TRANSFORMATION \longrightarrow OUTPUT$$

INPUTS	OUTPUT
people	goods (tangibles)
money	services (intangibles)
machines	
technology	
entrepreneurship	

$- ADDING\ VALUE\ - - - - - - - - - - - - - - - - - - - \longrightarrow$

The success of a business can be measured in terms of the value it adds during the transaformation process, ie the extent to which the value of the sold or exchanged outputs is greater than the value of the inputs used up to produce them. If we are measuring success in financial terms, this means measuring the extent to which the revenue exceeds the costs, ie the extent to which a profit is made. In others cases it may not be appropriate to measure the outcomes in financial terms. For example, a hospital might want to measure waiting lists, bed usage or survival rates; a sixth-form college may look at its examination results.

The more successful the firm, the more value it can add; the more it can increase the positive difference between the value of the sold outputs and the inputs. This may be achieved by increasing efficiency so that less inputs are used up, or by providing a good or service that people are willing to pay more for.

It's a question of perspective

Exactly what business is, what it does or what determines its success, depends a great deal on our own individual perspectives. To some the main focus of business is the buyer. According to the business guru Peter Drucker, for example, the one and only aim of business is to 'create and maintain a customer'. Get this right and everything else, such as profits, follows. To others, the emphasis should be much more on the technical side of things. Ask a research and development manager what business is about and she would probably say it was to do with innovation and continually enhancing the product. Ask some chief executives what business is about and they may well say 'our people are our greatest asset – it's the people who make or break this thing called business'. So what seems to matter most and what seems to generate results depends on who you ask. Accountants are more likely to focus on the importance of numbers, operations managers may stress the importance of production and marketers may claim it all comes down to the brand. Similarly, if you were trying to describe the way in which businesses behaved, you would get very different answers depending on who you asked. Anyone's view of business depends heavily on their own contact with different organisations. If you work for a huge multinational such as Exxon or General Motors, business may be seen in terms of massive armies facing each other head-on across the world. If you have set up your own business, you may think it is more about guerilla warfare – winning by attacking larger organisations in ways and in markets they least expect.

There are many routes to success (and failure), and businesses come in all shapes and sizes. Don't always look for the essential truths – enjoy the variety and listen to people's views of business critically. You might want to compare different perspectives before you make up your own mind.

Summary points

▶ a business undertakes a transformation process and offers goods and services to a market. Business turns inputs into outputs

▶ don't just think of business in terms of profit-making enterprises; it also includes non-proft-making organisations such as charities

▶ each person's view of what a business does depends on which business they are looking at and their own perspective

▶ a business usually involves the following activities: marketing, people management, operations management, finance, innovation; however, the relative importance of these activities can vary

THINK about it!

Think about the organisation where you study or work, and write down the inputs used and outputs that are produced. Think about the nature of the transformation process that occurs. How would you measure the success of the organisation?

Business format

What's the difference between a 'business' and a 'company'?

Anyone can set up a business, but a company is something special in law. It has its own legal identity, it can buy and sell its own assets, and is responsible for its own liabilities. Imagine you set up as a plumber working on your own as a sole trader. If anything goes wrong and you flood someone's house, you have unlimited liability. This means that you are personally responsible for the activities of the business and, as a result, you could lose all of your own savings. Alternatively you could set up a company, such as 'Jack's Plumbing Ltd'. To do this, you have to fill in various forms and register your business with Companies House. This will give your business limited liability status, meaning that the company is now responsible for its own actions. If Jack's Plumbing Ltd floods a house the company can be taken to court and could lose all its assets, BUT the owners cannot lose their personal savings. Imagine you invested £100 into a company – if the company had financial difficulties you might lose this £100 but no more. Your life savings are safe.

Having limited liability is crucial for companies – it allows them to attract investors. If you didn't have the knowledge that your house and savings were safe you would be unlikely to put money into companies when, on a day-to-day basis, you had relatively little control over what the managers were doing. But if you know the very worst that could happen is that you could lose your initial investment you are much more likely to take the risk. Limited liability allows companies to raise more finance and grow more rapidly than if they relied on financing everything internally or on friends and family.

So why doesn't everyone set up a company?

In some cases, it's not really necessary. If all you do is to give after-dinner talks, the likelihood of you being sued is fairly minimal. Also, setting up as a company is not as easy as filling in a series of forms. In return for having limited liability, a company must produce annual reports showing its assets and its profits. If you are a sole trader working for yourself, the only person you have to tell your income to is the taxman. If you are a company, your profit figures are available for everyone to see. You may not want to lose your privacy, so becoming a company may be unattractive.

There are in fact two types of company: a 'ltd' and a 'plc'. A ltd is a private company which cannot advertise its shares, whereas a plc is a public limited company which can advertise its shares and trade on the Stock Exchange (which is basically just a big market place for buyers and sellers). This means that plcs have access to far more potential investors; however, they are also subject to more regulation. For example, plcs have to publish far more information about their financial affairs than ltds. When a private limited company becomes a public limited company (ie offers its shares to the general public on the Stock Exchange), this is known as a 'flotation'.

Keeping it in the family

Over 75% of companies remain very closely controlled by their founding families. Even many large organisations such as BMW, Ford, Mars and JCB have a strong family influence. This brings with it particular strengths: family loyalties can be a strong powerful force and lead to a 24-hour, 365-day-a-year commitment to the firm's success that an outsider may find difficult to match. Also, traditionally, family companies are willing and able to take a long- term view. They are more willing to reinvest and do not have to compromise their strategy to pressures from outside investors. According to Mr Agnelli (whose family has a big share of Fiat), there is 'A continuity born of the belief that the company is an inheritance to be protected and handed on. It is the outcome of each generation's commitment to the next and each generation's commitment to the last... This implies a determination – that may at times border on the reckless – not to give up when the going gets tough and to do everything humanly possible to protect the business from the dangers of political and economic instability'.

This is not to say that family firms lack problems – far from it. In particular, when you get to the second and third generations there may be a big difference in views about where to take the business next. Abbott and Hay[1] have shown that the growth rates of family firms tend to slow as successive generations inherit the company and seek to 'harvest' the business. This has led to some fairly high-profile family disputes (eg, within the Moores family which owns Littlewoods, the Clark family which owns the shoe company and the Blackwell family which owns a large bookshop and publishing company). The younger family members often want to float the business and turn it into a plc. That way they can sell their shares and turn their 'paper' into cash. Others may be more eager to keep the business private and within the family; this may mean that people are wealthy on paper but don't have the cash they might get if they could sell their shares on the Stock Exchange.

Summary points

▶ a company has its own legal identity

▶ a company has limited liability which is extremely important for investors because it provides some protection for their personal assets

▶ there are two types of company: a private limited company (ltd) and a public limited company (plc)

▶ the downside of forming a company is that it is more regulated than a sole trader

A friend of yours, Joanna, has always made her own jewellery, selling it to friends and family. Recently, orders for her products have grown and she has gained a lot of new customers. She has asked you whether she should form a company or not. Identify three key factors you would need to know before deciding. Under what circumstances would you recommend her to go ahead?

Franklin Mints Chocolates have been produced by Franklin Limited for nearly 85 years. The company is still owned by the family with Charles, the great-grandson of the founder, now the Chief Executive. In the last year there have been disputes amongst family members about what to do with the company – some want to float it and turn it into a public limited company. Charles is an old friend and has asked for your opinion. Identify three factors Charles should take into account when deciding whether to float or not. Under what circumstances would you advise Charles to go ahead?

Shareholders

Why buy a share?

If you buy a share in a company, you become an owner of the business. Although there are different types of shares, a shareholder typically has one vote per share. The more shares you have the more votes you get. So if you have 51% of the shares you have control of the business. In reality, given that ownership is often spread quite widely amongst many different shareholders, anyone with ownership of even 10% of the total number is relatively powerful (imagine owning 10% of Microsoft!). The actual day-to-day running of the business is left to the managers. The shareholders and managers may be the same people, particularly in smaller firms, but in large organisations they are often different. This is known as a divorce between ownership and control.

Given that there may be thousands of shareholders, there needs to be some way that they maintain control over the managers. This is done via the board of directors. The directors are elected by shareholders to meet fairly regularly and supervise the actions of the managers. They act as a watchdog for investors. The shareholders are then invited to an Annual General Meeting where the results are presented and they can ask questions.

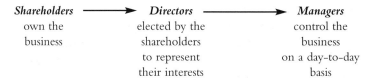

Shareholders	→	*Directors*	→	*Managers*
own the business		elected by the shareholders to represent their interests		control the business on a day-to-day basis

However, there is always the danger that the business is not being run in the shareholders' best interests. The managers may well be pursuing their own goals, taking decisions to further their own careers rather than to boost the value of the company and it is difficult for the shareholders to know. In the 1990s (and even now) there were real concerns in many organisations that 'fat cat' managers and directors were increasing their own salaries at the expense of shareholders. There was particular anger at the pay of the chief executives of privatised utilities, such as Cedric Brown at British Gas – 51% of shareholders voted to oust Brown in March 1995 when he was awarded a phenomenal pay increase even though the company's profits were dropping. In 2000, Greg Hutchings, chief executive of Tomkins plc, resigned over complaints about corporate excess including the use of four private jets, several flats and lavish parties.

The problem with allowing the managers and directors to run the business on behalf of the shareholders is that there is an imbalance of information – the average shareholder has limited insight into the business and so there has to be a degree of trust in those appointed to serve them well. In some cases this trust is definitely abused – in 1991 Robert Maxwell, a very well known and flamboyant business figure of the time, was found to have misled shareholders and lenders about the financial affairs of the Mirror Group (which published the *Daily Mirror* newspaper). He had also misused the pension funds, leaving pensioners without their savings. Maxwell died in a boating accident before he could be brought to court.

Part of the problem is that many directors are also managers in the company. This means they are supposedly checking themselves on behalf of the shareholders! Probably not the most effective system you could devise. To overcome this problem, investigating committees set up by the government, such as the Cadbury and Greenbury Committees, have recommended that boards of directors make greater use of non-executive directors, ie they bring in more people from outside the company to monitor the management. The current codes of conduct include recommendations such as:

- all directors should be subject to election at least every three years
- one-third of the Board should be made up of non-executive directors.

The rewards of owning shares

The financial rewards of ownership mainly come via increases in the share price and dividends. The share price will reflect the perceived value of the company and is determined by supply and demand. The more shares on the market the less each one represents in terms of ownership of the business and so the less it will be worth. If a £100 m company is divided into 100 million shares, each one should be worth £1. If it is divided into 200 million shares, each one should be worth 50 pence. But what determines whether the overall company is worth £100 m or £300 m? This is all in the eyes of the beholder – an organisation's value depends on what people are willing to pay for it. This can change within minutes as more information comes out about a new product being developed, a key manager leaving or a change in the economy. This is why share prices can be very volatile. It is also why the views of analysts and newspapers are so important – if they like a company and write about it favourably, this may boost the share price.

The dividends are the payments from the firm's profits to its owners. The amount paid out will depend on the size of the company's profits, what other firms are paying and the long-run strategy of the firm. The more you pay out now the less you have for investment. So the pay out also depends on whether your shareholders want their money now or whether they can wait.

Get off my back

Shareholders provide the investment necessary to start up a company, and they are likely to be asked to put more money in at various stages during its development to finance its expansion. Not surprisingly, in return they usually want a say in how the business is run, to use their votes and influence what the managers do. Of course this is their right, given that they do in fact own the business, but it can be somewhat irritating for managers who are trying to get on with the daily operations of the business. The last thing many managers want is hoards of shareholders asking difficult questions and wanting them to explain everything that is going on. If the managers can limit the feedback they have to give in an annual report and annual general meeting, then all the better (at least that's what many of them think!). However, if particular shareholders have enough votes they can make their presence felt on a regular basis and insist on the policies and direction the business takes.

In the case of entrepreneurs who have set up their own business and then watched it grow with the help of outside investors, the 'interference' of shareholders can be a real issue. Entrepreneurs are likely to still regard the business as their own, even if they have long since lost the controlling interest. For example, Richard Branson, Andrew Lloyd Webber and Alan Sugar have had fairly heated disagreements with their shareholders over the future direction of their businesses. In the case of the first two they eventually bought back the business because they wanted it under their own control again.

Who are the shareholders in the UK?

The main shareholders in UK plcs are financial institutions such as pension funds. These institutions have their own shareholders to answer to, and tend to be interested in the ability of a company to provide short-term returns. Compare this with other countries such as Japan and Germany, where the shareholders tend to be partners with the business in some way. For example a firm's suppliers, its sub-contractors or its banks may lend it money; this type of shareholder tends to be more willing to wait for returns and to be interested in the long-term success of the business. It should be easier to explain to them why investment in brand building or new technology may be necessary, compared to a typical UK investor looking for a quick way to make money.

Summary points

- a shareholder is an owner of the company

- the more shares you have, the more votes you have and the greater control you have over the company

- the share price of a company depends on the number of shares available and the demand for them

- the dividends are the amount paid out of profits each year to shareholders; the more that is paid out, the less there is left for investment

- the directors are elected by the shareholders to protect their interests (in theory!)

- most shares in the UK are owned by financial institutions

For the last few months the share price of Eltectron plc, an advertising agency, has been rising. The company has been highly praised in the media for its innovative work and has grown rapidly. You have £20,000 of savings ready to invest in shares. What would you want to know before buying shares in Eltectron plc? What are the three key questions you would ask the managing director if you met her? Why these questions?

Starting up is hard to do

At one time or another, many of us have thought of starting up our own business. Thoughts of making all our own decisions and being in charge of all we survey is naturally appealing. There is something attractive about taking risks, finding new ways of doing things and creating something for yourself. Just think of the rewards you can earn or the pride you can get from building up a business.

- Charles Dunstone set up 'The Carphone Warehouse' in 1989 with just £6,000; 11 years later it was floated on the London Stock Exchange and valued at almost £1.9 bn!

- In 1975 Bill Gates and Paul Allen set up Microsoft. By 2000 the company was making over $9 bn in profit, and Gates alone was worth over £37 bn.

- At the age of 13, twins Philip and Andrew Oliver started developing computer games in their bedroom. They went on to set up *Blitz*, creator of games such as 'Chicken Run' and 'The Mummy Returns', providing games for *Sony*'s Playstation 1 and 2, *Nintendo*'s Gamecube and *Microsoft*'s Xbox.

Entrepreneurship

However, while these rewards are certainly attractive, only a few entrepreneurs are this successful, and success rarely comes easily. The reality is that starting your own business is hard work – it involves stress, pressure from all sides and a juggling act to keep all aspects of the business on track. Many people find they have let themselves in for far more than they had bargained for once they set up on their own. They go into business because they love selling or producing or researching and then find that they have to do lots of other things as well.

To find a true entrepreneur in the UK look no further than Sir Terence Conran: designer, restauranteur and retailer. Visit Butler's Wharf on the south bank of the river Thames in London and you'll find a Conran coffee kiosk, a Conran wine merchant, a Conran bakery and four Conran restaurants. He also produces *Conran* magazine as well as being a furniture designer and maker! Conran has been at the cutting edge of British design for over 40 years: his store Habitat captured much of the essence of the 1960s in the UK and Conran has been a prominent business figure since then.

Another successful UK entrepreneur is Bill Archer who became chairman and founder of Britain's biggest independent do-it-yourself retailer. Archer's success has been helped by the fascination the British public has with television programmes such as *Home Front* and *Changing Rooms*, which involve makeovers of homes and gardens. For Archer such market developments enabled an initial investment of £300,000 to be turned into a fortune of at least £300 m (which is what his stake in Focus was worth around the end of 2001).

All over the country, people like Conran and Archer (or wanting to be like them!) are setting up businesses, trying out new ideas and providing goods and services for customers. The economy is made up of thousands of people engaged in commercial activity, providing countless goods and services and at the heart of these organisations are the entrepreneurs that set up new businesses and build new empires. They take the risk to invest time, energy and money to create something different, whether it be a new restaurant, a new computer game or a new fashion.

- In 1965, Alan Sugar started selling reconditioned TV sets from his home in Hackney. He went on to set up Amstrad, selling personal computers and

more recently the em@ailer; he also acquired Viglen computers and for a while had a 40% stake in Tottenham Hotspur football club.
- Richard Branson started selling records while still at school, and went on to create countless companies under the Virgin brand name, including an airline, a train company, a credit card business, a music business.

But what drives these entrepreneurs? Are they different from the rest of us in some way or are we all capable of such success?

According to the business writer Deakins[2], the main personality characteristics of entrepreneurs are:
- the need for achievement – entrepreneurs want to do something to be someone
- the desire to be in control of their environment and destiny – they want to be their own boss
- a willingness to take risks
- the need to be independent
- an unconventional personality – they do not feel comfortable in a large firm
- a capacity for innovation.

So, what do you think – do you have the skills to succeed?

Summary points

▶ starting a business requires a range of skills and commitment many of us may not have; just having the idea is not enough

▶ being an entrepreneur may suit some personalities more than others, eg it may suit those who have a real desire for achievement and a willingness to take risks

An old friend and business partner, Hildegard Henshaw, has approached with you a 'brilliant new business idea with incredible potential' (her words!). She is looking for investors to help get the project started. Imagine you can ask her three questions before deciding whether to invest. What would you ask her? Why did you choose these questions?

How not to do it

There are many challenges facing start-up businesses. Entrepreneurs often have to learn a lot of different skills quickly and cope with getting the business up and running despite all the problems with legislation, planning permission and so on. Even if the idea is good the business has to be managed properly from the very beginning.

Why do businesses fail?

As you can imagine, every person who has lost their business has their own story to tell. The reason for each failed business is in some way unique. But having said this there are some common themes. In many cases, it is because the entrepreneurs failed to manage the cash properly. The idea may have been fine but the timing of the inflows and outflows did not match. Often the entrepreneur tried to grow too fast and ended up with too much money tied up in stocks or property, and/or lacked the power to chase up the money they were owed.

Another common problem is that the marketing was inappropriate. The product was not quite as different as they had thought; the competition was stronger than they expected; the demand did not come in at the rate they had hoped. Production problems can also be an issue, eg products are sometimes rushed to the market before they are fully tested. This is quite common in markets such as the software industry where the pressure to innovate is intense.

Failure, it seems, can come from many different directions, which is why it is so important to keep informed and flexible.

Boo.com – rise and fall

A good example of how not to start up a business is Boo.com. This supposed star in the world of dot.coms was all set to light up the world and show the potential of e-commerce. As it turned out, it highlighted the fragile nature of such businesses and the problems that occur when those at the top are not effective managers.

Boo.com was set up by Ernst Malmsten and Kajsa Leander. Having built up and sold one small online bookseller in Sweden, the pair moved to London and raised millions for Boo.com. Their view was that fashion is global, that it offers high profit margins and that its consumers are young and online – a perfect opportunity for e-commerce.

Malmsten and Leander were certainly good at public relations and even managed to make the cover of *Fortune* magazine. Unfortunately, instead of focusing on getting the business ready on time and on budget the two seemed more intent on talking at conferences in Venice, shooting TV commercials in Los Angeles and spending $10,000 on clothes. They held staff parties in smart nightclubs before the company even had a product, and flew around the world to investor meetings on Concorde and private jets. Five different deadlines for launch were set and missed so that when the site did finally open it was five months later than planned.

Boo.com was eventually launched in seven languages in 18 countries including America, but the site was so high tech that only customers with state of the art equipment could use it! Most websites have a few pictures on them; Boo was more ambitious and had images of shoes and clothes spinning through 360°. Customers could even dress a model in their favourite outfits. Unfortunately this made the site far too slow for most users.

The huge advertising and technology cost the company dearly and expenses were running at $1 m a week. On the first day after the launch in November 1999 there were only 25,000 visits compared with the expected one million, and it was soon clear that sales would be less than one-tenth of the promised target of $37 m in the first seven months. Although sales did begin to pick up, time was running out. The company managed to find an additional $15 m but needed $25 m to stay afloat and out of insolvency.

It was liquidated on 17 May 2000, barely six months after its launch. The founders had spent about $100 m of investors money along the way! The company was eventually rescued by Fashionmail.com for a mere £250,000, but 18 months later this company announced it was also considering abandoning online retailing because it could not make any money from it.

Iridium – difficulties with the launch

Another example of a major business failure is Iridium, which was intended to offer a 'use anywhere' satellite phone service. The Iridium project envisaged a system of 77 low earth-orbit satellites (Iridium is the 77th chemical element, hence the name) connecting phone users. In 1993 Iridium raised $800 m in the first round of funding; at this time Motorola (a major investor) produced a business plan for Iridium that forecast two million users by 2002, with profits flowing even earlier.

However, in the run-up to the launch, it emerged that Iridium handsets would retail for about $3,000, while call rates would be up to $7 a minute. This was at a time when the cellular market was undergoing tremendous growth driven by falling handset prices and call rates. Iridium remained convinced that senior executives would be willing to pay a significant premium for the benefit of being able to make calls from anywhere in the world. Unfortunately, at the same time the Global System for Mobile (GSM) was becoming the international standard around the world outside the US, and with this came 'roaming agreements' that enabled users to use their mobile phones abroad – at once removing the Iridium 'use anywhere' advantage.

Other problems with the product included the fact that the Iridium handset weighed 500g (typically handsets now weighs 120g or less). The launch itself cost over $140 m and had to be delayed for six weeks due to 'technical problems'. When it did finally launch, the phones were in short supply and the customer support service was virtually non-existent. So here was an expensive bulky product with no clear advantage over the competition and with various technical difficulties – hardly a recipe for success.

ONDigital – from launch to bankruptcy within three years

In the late 1990s BDB (British Digital Broadcasting), a joint venture of Granada, Carlton and Sky, identified a business opportunity and put together a bid for the rights for digital terrestial television in the UK. However, this proposal was soon quashed by the EU competition regulators who would not allow Sky to take part because it was also offering a satellite service. As a result Sky pulled out of the deal, and Granada and Carlton made a bid for the licence to transmit under the name of ONDigital.

ONDigital was launched in November 1998 with a marketing budget of £80 m. The nature of the launch highlights just how precarious and risky the business world can be:

- amazingly the company could not accurately predict how many people could receive its broadcasts until it was actually turned on on the first day! It turned out that the reception was much weaker than imagined, significantly reducing the potential customer base
- one month before the ONDigital launch, Sky started to offer free set-top receiver boxes for its services. ONDigital had to match this offer by also offering its receivers free, and this completely destroyed its original business plan. Before launching it had assumed it would earn about £100 m income from the sale of the set-top boxes – now, thanks to Sky, it would earn nothing!

Within months ONDigital was in trouble with poor reception, far less income than expected and high levels of customer dissatisfaction. In an attempt to turn the business around, the company decided to bid for the rights to televise certain sports events. However, because ONDigital did not have much money to bargain with at this stage, it had to settle on the rights to the Nationwide football league First Division. In June 2000 the company agreed to pay £315 m for the rights for three years to televise these games. The problem was that very few people actually wanted to watch these matches! The rights cost about £1.2 m per match on average, but the number of viewers was typically only 1,000. It was calculated that it would have been cheaper to pick up every viewer in a taxi, drive them to the match and let them stay in a hotel for the night! In March 2002, the company called in the administrators to try and save the business because it was bankrupt.

The ONDigital story highlights:
- the difficulties firms can have in forecasting sales
- the dangers from unexpected competitors' actions
- how much can turn on one strategic decision – in this case the mistaken belief that First Division football would generate large numbers of viewers.

Back from the dead

The beauty of business is its ability to surprise. Just when you think you know what's happening, things change. Firms that seem bound to succeed falter and stumble. Others that seem on their last legs suddenly pick themselves up and bounce back. Take the Triumph motorbike business. In the 1970s Triumph suffered from poor management and failed rescue attempts by the government until it finally crashed in the early 1980s. The credit for Triumph's rebirth goes to John Bloor, a builder who bought the company in 1983. He invested £80m on, among other things, a new plant in Leicestershire, and completely revamped the product. New engines were crucial to the firm's revival; the new Triumphs had a 3-cylinder layout, making them more powerful than the 2-cylinder bikes made in Europe and more relaxing than the high-revving 4-cylinder bikes made in Japan – 3-cylinder engines were perfect for the target group of middle-aged men. Triumph's sales rose from 2,000 bikes in 1991 to 33,000 ten years later, bringing the old sales peak of 50,000 in the late 1960s back within sight. Most Triumph buyers are now aged between 35 and 55 and American sales (which make up 25% of total) are increasing at an impressive 40% pa.

Summary points

- some people get carried away when starting up a business (boo who?)
- businesses fail for a host of reasons, including cash-flow problems, poor marketing and technical problems with the product
- not all dying businesses have to die

Growing pains

You have an idea. You set up in business. It succeeds. The business grows. Life changes. In the beginning you can make all the decisions – you want something done so you do it, or someone else in the office does it for you. It happens quickly. If you don't like something you say so, you stop it. You are the master of your destiny. But the more business you do, the more you find yourself organising others rather than doing it yourself. You're not face-to-face with the customer anymore. You're more likely to spend your time with your managers or investors. Getting an answer about what is happening can take longer; decision-making is slower because more people need to be involved or consulted. For some entrepreneurs this can be a difficult experience – in some cases they will deliberately shrink the business back down so it is all under their control again. Others make the transition more smoothly.

Jim Clark – a genius who fought with his investors

Jim Clark is an American billionaire who has made his money through computer technology. Clark set up the company Silicon Graphics (SGI) that developed the technology that allows PCs to use 3D graphics. His technology made it possible to design almost anything on computer, and soon interested firms as diverse as Hollywood film companies and aircraft designers. Clark assembled an amazing team of engineers – people wanted to work for him because of the cutting edge technology he was working on.

But as the business grew and more investors became involved, Clark became irritated by their interference and the fact that many of the rewards were going to them, not him and his team of engineers. In order to get the finance to develop the technology, Clark had to give up more and more ownership of his company. A huge rift developed between the investors (and the 'managers' they appointed) and the engineers like Clark. Clark and his team wanted to make the most technically advanced equipment they could even though it cost a lot to develop and would probably be too expensive and too powerful for most of their customers! The managers just wanted something they could sell.

Differences between the two camps became so fierce that the Chief Executive Ed McCracken, who had been appointed by the outside investors, hired a corporate psychologist to test Clark and his team. The results described Clark and his engineers as 'highly oppositional'. Clark became so upset at not being listened to when that he simply stopped turning up for work. He went on to make another fortune setting up Netscape.

Ben and Jerry – having to let go

The experience of Ben and Jerry's ice cream company also highlights the problems of coping with a business which gradually becomes the responsibility of other people. Here were two high school graduates who identified a market opportunity for luxury ice cream. A good product, an innovative approach to business and superb public relations led to a huge growth in sales, with the end result that the founders gradually became less and less involved with the day-to-day running of the company. Of course this means they have many new challenges as they are invited on to numerous committees and asked for their opinion by all sorts of important bodies, but it also means they are removed from what they originally liked doing: making ice cream. As more investors are brought in, the founders lose some control over what was their creation.

As Ben and Jerry themselves say: 'It's difficult to be involved in a business at a high level, to be the founders of a business, and not always to be in agreement with some of the decisions that your business makes. Friends who have teenage kids and teenage companies like ours tell us that the two experiences are a lot alike. For years you've got these children who are totally dependent on you, totally under your control. They wear the clothes you put on them and go wherever you take them. Then one day they're taller and stronger than you are. They're buying their own clothes and driving their own cars. They have their own ideas about everything and a lot of them aren't the same as yours.'

Summary points

▶ growth can be exciting but it can also be tough

▶ you may end up with something which you no longer control and which is very different from the thing you set up

▶ success can therefore bring with it its own problems: you may have to talk to lots of analysts and journalists when you want to be running your business; you may have to listen to outside investors; you may lose the personal contact with customers

You run a small bookshop in Oxford. You bought the premises nine years ago and have built up a good local customer base. A bookshop in Witney (about 10 miles away) has recently gone on the market and you are interested in buying it. Identify three key factors which would help you decide whether or not to buy the other shop.

Stages of growth

Even if the founders of a company want the business to grow and can cope with the personal changes this can bring, success usually requires a change in the whole structure of the organisation. It is important, as an organisation grows, that the over-reliance on the entrepreneur is removed and a proper structure is built with people who can hold up the organisation for themselves. It also requires that jobs are more closely defined so that individuals know what to do and there is less danger of overlap.

In a small business individuals are likely to see each other regularly and be able to sort out who is doing what amongst themselves. As the firm grows this is not possible (people on are different sites and not seeing each other as often) – roles need much more formal definition. This change in the way the business is run usually involves a move from a power culture to a role culture (see page 63).

Typical problems that occur as a business grows include:
- **communication** – more outlets or bases involve more geographical distance between people, making communication harder. Information technology can help, but nothing can replace the value of regular face-to-

face contact. As the firm grows and acquires more staff this tends to create more layers of hierarchy; this in turn creates more layers for messages to pass through and therefore more opportunities for messages to be distorted.

- **control** – imagine you are managing General Electric with several hundred thousand employees worldwide; how do you keep this workforce focused and working towards the same objectives? How do you maintain any sense of identify and belonging between Charlene in Idaho, USA and Carol in Oxfordshire, UK? You can use training, a system of management by objectives, newsletters, corporate videos, share options and so on, but this is no easy task.
- **morale** – it is easy for subcultures to develop in large organisations and for groups and teams to form their own views of what matters, what is acceptable and what they are aiming for; these views do not necessarily correlate with what senior management is thinking

Greiner's model

Greiner's model highlights several stages of growth and the challenges these then bring for many firms as they expand:

Greiner's model

The five stages identified in Greiner's model[3] are:

- *growth through creativity leading to a crisis of leadership* – an entrepreneur takes risks and sets up a business. The business is driven by the founder's creativity. However, as the firm grows it becomes increasingly difficult for the entrepreneur to control the business. There is too much to do and the workload becomes unmanageable. This causes a leadership crisis as the business lacks the firm hand at the helm.
- *growth through direction leading to a crisis of autonomy* – to overcome the crisis of leadership, the organisation needs to appoint professional managers and introduce more formal procedures. Specialists are often brought in and a

more formal approach is adopted. However, with further growth these professionals want more independence in their own areas. Central control becomes resisted as managers want the freedom to make more decisions in their part of the business.

■ *growth through delegation leading to a crisis of control* – to overcome the crisis of autonomy the senior managers have to delegate more and loosen the central control. The problem with this as the organisation continues to grow is that there are too many divisions and departments pulling in different directions. This can lead to a crisis of control.

■ *growth through coordination leading to a crisis of red tape* – facing problems controlling the business means more effort has to be put into developing appropriate coordinating mechanisms. The problem with this is that it can lead to too many groups and committees. Complexity replaces control.

■ *growth through collaboration – crisis of ???? (uncertainty)* – to overcome the problem of too much red tape, greater emphasis can be placed on the initiative and self-control of well-trained managers. In such mature organisation the formal structure may be seen as less important. However, there is always likely to be a crisis of some (if yet unknown) form in the future.

Wal-Mart: bucking the trend?

Although Greiner's model illustrates many problems that can occur at different stages of a firm's development, this does not mean that successful growth is impossible. Just take a look at Wal-Mart, a true retailing giant. The first Wal-Mart shop was set up by Sam Walton in 1962 in a small town near Bentonville, USA, because retailers such as K-mart and Sears dominated the large towns. Wal-Mart now has a turnover of more than $215 bn, and with 1.2 million staff it is the largest private sector employer of staff in the world. Its skills and power enable it to enter and dominate markets fairly quickly. For example, in 1995 it sold almost no food; by 2001 it was America's biggest grocer retailer!

So how does Wal-Mart manage its growth so successfully? The answer is that despite its huge size the company still manages to retain a paternalistic feel. All employees at Wal-Mart are called 'associates'. Most own shares and take part in profit-sharing schemes; many have become millionaires as a result. They have quite a large degree of independence – managers are given lots of information of present and past performance and have the power to make decisions for themselves. Even the most junior employee can change the price of something if it is cheaper elsewhere; after all, the company promises 'everyday low prices'. This kind of approach means that employees still see themselves as part of the whole organisation and are willing to adopt its values, but are also flexible enough to react to local conditions.

Wal-Mart now accounts for an incredible 60% of America's retail sales. Its store sales growth is five times the industry average and its profits reached an astounding $9.3 bn in 2000. However, it still wants to expand even more. Given that further growth within the US may be difficult, expansion is likely to come from overseas. Wal-Mart is already the biggest retailer in Mexico and Canada, and by buying Asda in the UK for $6.7 bn it became number three there. It is now targeting China.

Methods of growth: takeover and merger

Some firms grow internally, building up their own sales. Others go on the prowl and snap up other businesses; this is external growth through acquisition (eg the Royal Bank of Scotland bought National Westminster in February 2000 for £21 bn and Vodafone bought Mannesmann in 2000 for £112 bn). To bring off a takeover, you need to gain a controlling interest in another company's shares. In the case of a plc there are no restrictions on who the shares are sold to, so if you offer the right price you may get your way. In the case of a private limited company restrictions can be placed on the sale of shares (eg they may be sold to family members only), so this type of company can be more difficult to gain control of.

To buy another company's shares the aggressor may either offer cash or some of its own shares (this is called a 'paper offer'). The Board of Directors of the victim company will respond to this offer and recommend to their shareholders whether or not they think they should sell. This will depend on whether they think the price is right and whether they think the bid is in the best interests of the business. In 1986 when BTR made a bid for Pilkington plc, the latter successfully argued that BTR would asset-strip and destroy the firm's strengths in areas such as research and development. Of course it is up to the shareholders themselves whether they listen. In the case of Pilkington they did, and the company successfully fought off the takeover bid.

An alternative to this type of external growth is to merge the companies. This is a voluntary union and less risky than a takeover in that the two companies are likely to share information about their relative strengths; in the case of a takeover you may not be entirely sure what you are bidding for. You have the balance sheet to go on, but this is not necessarily very informative because of window dressing.

Why pursue external growth?

In theory there are good logical economic reasons for many takeovers. For example, growth can bring about economies of scale and market power. However, although outwardly appealing for many reasons, many takeovers and mergers actually turn out to be much less successful than originally imagined. In particular there are often culture clashes and inefficiency because of problems of trying to coordinate a larger organisation. Sudden growth like this must be handled very carefully. Takeovers can also be very expensive, making it difficult for the new business to recover the premium paid to make the bid successful.

One of the largest mergers in recent years was between AOL and Time Warner in 1999. This created a multi-media company with a market value of over $200 bn and included Warner films, Warner records, *Time* magazine, CNN, and AOL online services. One of the reasons behind it was 'synergy' – the benefits of sharing resources and the idea that together the two firms would be much stronger than they are individually. For example, when Madonna (who is signed to the Warner Brothers record label) went on her world tour, this was promoted on AOL; the tour was also televised and shown on the group's pay-per-view television channel. According to Bob Pittman, co-Chief Operating Officer of the merged company, 'combining assets in one place gives you critical mass that allows you to take risks'.

However, the merger has not been without its difficulties. The two companies headquarters (AOL's in northern Virginia and Time Warner's in Manhattan) were 200 miles apart and there was a huge cultural gap between the restless younger AOL staff and the more establishment characters at Time Inc that owns titles such as *Sports Illustrated* and *Fortune* magazine.

Ventures

If you don't want a full-blown takeover or merger, you might go for an alliance or venture. These are quite common when firms have skills in particular fields that they want to share, or where they want to collaborate on specific issues but do not want to be joined at the hip. For example, it may be that you have a good distribution network in the UK and someone else has good access to outlets in France. If you share your contacts and resources you can both benefit. Alternatively, you may have a good idea but lack the necessary development facilities – a larger partner may be able to provide this. Ventures may also be the way into a market: in some countries access to the market is only possible via a local producer.

Is big beautiful?

There has been much discussion in both economics and business about the ideal size of a firm. Is big truly beautiful, or are smaller firms best suited to survive and succeed?

There are, of course, advantages both to being large and being small. Large firms are likely to have more influence in the market; they can probably influence suppliers more easily, absorb shocks and negotiate better rates with the media. Small firms, by comparison, can usually react more quickly to change, can pick out niches in a market and in many cases are more innovative. The appeal of large size lies partly in the power and the status. For managers and owners, it also offers more profit and more financial rewards as well as providing some sense of progression. Anyone who takes on a business is going to be tempted to try and expand it; growth is perceived as a natural objective.

The ideal size

The ideal size of a firm will depend on a number of factors, including:

- the ability of a firm to control and coordinate a larger scale business. This will in turn depend on the way it is organised, the way IT is used and the commitment to good communication
- the personal objectives of owners – how important is large size to them?
- the benefits of large scale – are the unit costs much lower by buying, producing, marketing and transporting on a larger scale?
- how big is the market? There's no point producing if the product is not going to sell!

Summary points

- as firms grow they are likely to encounter a series of crises concerning control and coordination

- despite such difficulties, some firms manage to cope well – ask Wal-Mart!

- external growth is quick but risky; some firms prefer the slower pace of internal growth

- both large and small scale have good points; owners and managers must choose what it right for them and for the market conditions

- just because you are big does not mean you are necessarily safe from the competition; every firm is vulnerable, however big

You are the chief executive of Handel plc, a producer of industrial freezers. You have been approached by the managing director of a smaller competitor who wants to sell her business. Identify three main factors that would determine whether or not you make an offer for the business.

References

1. S. Abbott and M. Hay 'The Pulse Survey – Survival of the fittest' (Arthur Andersen and Binder Hamlyn, 1996)
2. David Deakins *Entrepreneurship and Small Firms* (McGraw Hill, 1996)
3. L.E. Greiner 'Evolution and revolutions as organisations grow' *Harvard Business Review* Vol 50.4 (1972)

Objectives, strategy and management

Mission and objectives

Who are we? What do we do?

These are the key questions every organisation should ask itself on a regular basis. It may seem very obvious – we make soup, we sell insurance, we print books. But it's always worth standing back and thinking carefully about what you actually do. Are you really selling soup, or are you selling relaxation after a hard day's work? Are you selling books or are you providing access to information?

Why does it matter? Well, if you don't really know *exactly* what you are, you probably are not doing it very well. Imagine you define yourself as a company that provides roadside assistance to motorists – you naturally focus on a quick response time and effective service. If, however, you take a broader view and see yourself as 'an organisation that helps travellers to get from A to B', this opens up all sorts of possibilities and new ways of thinking:

- What about providing maps and information to help motorists avoid traffic jams?
- What about an advice service on the best route to choose or the best places to stay en route?
- What about non-motorists, eg cyclists – can you develop a service for them?
- What about travel insurance?

A wider view of what you are and what you do may take you into new markets.

The importance of understanding who you really are can be seen in the story of Parker Pens. Many years ago Parker Pens undertook a study of its market to try and understand how it was perceived by its customers. What were potential customers buying if they were not buying Parker Pens? The answer may seem simple: Parker makes pens; if people don't buy its pens, they buy Bic or Schaeffer. In reality many people saw Parker as a company that provided gifts they could buy for their children or grandchildren or their nephews or nieces. When the children are about to go back to school or when they have a birthday, a Parker pen was a possible present. Therefore the competition was not necessarily other pens but other gifts. Redefining itself, Parker developed a new range of pens and changed the emphasis in its marketing. They targeted more gift shops and paid greater attention to issues such as the packaging and gift-wrapping.

In the 1980s, many football clubs underwent a transformation as they began to appreciate that they were actually entertainment providers rather than just sports providers. People went to watch a match, but they were also interested in the whole experience – how to get to the ground, how long they have to wait to get in, the conditions inside, the food, the entertainment before the match, the shopping opportunities and so on. That's why clubs have built hotels near or actually as part of the grounds, and why, for example, Manchester United has developed the brand so much that the club makes huge sums from merchandising. Football is big business and it's much more than kicking a ball these days.

IBM used to think of itself of as a company that made computers. The trouble with this view is that there are lots of firms making computers; ultimately the profit margins on this sort of product are going to be relatively small. All you are doing is putting together various bits such as circuit boards and monitors. So if competing in this type of market is particularly fierce and open to almost anyone who can finance a new factory, how can you make sure you win? What IBM has done is to look at its particular strengths and what it thinks it can do better than anyone else. It has years of experience in the industry and this knowledge is difficult for other firms to imitate or acquire quickly. IBM now positions itself as a provider of solutions – rather than just selling computers it sells advice and information which helps you to solve your IT problems. It saves you money and helps you do your business more effectively so you are happy to pay for the service.

Ground control to organisation: what is your mission?

The mission of a firm is the reason for its existence – it is the reason why it is there in the first place. Your mission may be to make a fortune, be famous, be happy or be all three. A firm's mission may be to be the world's largest manufacturer of chocolate, to be innovative or to be a low-cost provider.

The mission is often written down in the form of a formal mission statement. The statement usually includes the firm's vision of its future, details about where the business is competing and what it values. Look at the abbreviated mission statement of the South Yorkshire Police (on the following page) produced by Johnson and Scholes in their book, *Exploring Corporate Strategy*.[1]

> **SOUTH YORKSHIRE POLICE**
>
> Purpose:
> - To uphold the rule of law
> - To keep the Queen's peace
> - To prevent and detect crime
> - To protect life and to help and reassure people in need
>
> Values:
> - Act within the law, serving with integrity the ends of justice
> - Act fairly and reasonably without fear or favour and without prejudice of any kind
> - Be honest, courteous and tactful in all that we do and say
> - Ensure that the rights of all citizens are safeguarded regardless of status, race, colour, religion, sex or social background

Having a mission makes good sense. If you don't have a clear aim and a clear set of values then you probably don't know where you're going or how to behave. And, if you don't, it is highly unlikely anyone else will! As Goethe, a famous author, once wrote, 'It is not where we have been which matters but where we are going'. You may think you are trying to do one thing, while others think they're trying to achieve something completely different. Result? Conflict and inefficiency.

A mission statement

Provided it is expressed properly, having a *mission statement* (ie a written version of your mission) can be helpful. But the real question is whether the mission statement accurately reflects what the firm is trying to achieve and whether employees genuinely believe in it. If they do it will help them focus and decide on their priorities. The mission statement can directly affect how employees behave. Imagine you are in charge of a school: do you think your mission is to achieve good exam results, or to provide a good all-round education? They may not be the same thing. Your decision will have a big impact on what the teachers do in their lessons.

Despite the obvious appeal of mission statements, many firms seem to have adopted them almost because they would feel left out if they didn't. They've done it because everyone else has, not because they really understood their value. Unfortunately, simply writing down what you would like to be doesn't actually bring it about, particularly if you don't support the statement with appropriate action and resources. If you really want to be the best, be the biggest, be the most innovative you've got to 'walk the talk'. This will require real investment and commitment.

An effective mission statement will therefore reflect the values and behaviour of the organisation. It will show what the firm genuinely regards as important and what it genuinely wants to be. A 'fake' mission, by comparison, can do more harm than good – it is likely to be mocked and will reduce enthusiasm for any other management statements and initiatives about where the business is heading.

Summary points

- ▶ it's worth thinking about why you exist – it may not be the reason you thought

- ▶ a mission is the reason why an organisation exists; producing a mission statement can help employees to focus on where the organisation is heading in the future

- ▶ if it fails to reflect what genuinely happens within the organisation, a mission may undermine employees' confidence in the management

 **THINK about it!**

Think about the organisation where you work or study. If it already has a mission statement, get hold of a copy and decide whether or not this accurately reflects the vision and objectives of the organisation and the way it operates. If there is not a statement at the moment (or you do not think the existing one is good enough!), write one which you think would be appropriate. Keep the statement to a maximum of 15 lines.

What's your objective in this?

The mission sets out the general direction in which a firm wants to go, but does not define any specific targets. This is where objectives come in.

Objectives are the quantifiable targets that firms set for themselves. In some cases these are explicitly stated – managers make it clear they want to achieve X by Y – in order to coordinate actions and motivate staff to achieve the targets. Discussion about where the firm is going will help focus minds on what is happening and provide a sense of direction.

All for profit?

Typically we assume that the overriding objective of most businesses is profit. Of course this is only really relevant in the commercial sector; organisations such as charities, libraries and the police force are bound to have other objectives.

But why is profit so desirable? One reason is that it provides funds for more investment, so more profit can be acquired. It also provides rewards for the owners such as dividends, and hopefully increases the value of the business. In addition, it measures in financial terms whether the sold output of the business is worth more than the inputs used up to produce them. If an activity is not profitable, why bother doing it?

However, profit may not be a short-term objective – it may be a long-term goal. Take most start-up businesses: the founder's first objective is usually to survive, to prove the idea works. Once that is achieved (and it may take years if it happens at all), the process of acquiring profit really begins. Internet companies such as lastminute.com are literally taking years to get close to profits, as are many biotechnology companies. They are in it for the long haul. Meanwhile they are successfully employing people, providing a service and no doubt providing a great deal of pleasure to the founders (along with no small amount of pain now and again). Business keeps you busy, and it gives you status; that's why growth is often an objective along with (even instead of) profit. If it can bring in the money as well, all the better. There may be a whole host of other reasons why people start up and persevere with business. Samuel Goldwyn, the legendary Hollywood film producer, once said, 'If I were in this business only for the business, I wouldn't be in this business'.

So while profit is undoubtedly there as an objective for most organisations, it is usually intermingled with other factors such as growth, providing a service to society and so on. There may also be environmental or social objectives. Organisations may even be set up to benefit employees. Take the John Lewis Partnership – a large retail organisation that is owned by its employees (who are called 'partners'). In the words of its founder John Spedan Lewis, the 'supreme purpose' of the John Lewis Partnership 'is simply the happiness of its members'.

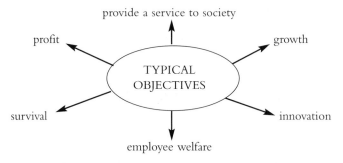

Where do objectives come from?

Next time you visit a business, look around at all the people running from meeting to meeting, armed with pens, computers, coffee and ideas. As you wander from office to office you will see people engaged with some project or another, talking intently, debating, discussing; all involved with making this enterprise work. So where do the objectives come from? From these huddles, these people arguing and considering where the business should be going next. They come from people who themselves have their own agendas. Imagine you are discussing with your friends where to go on Saturday. You have one idea, they have another. You haggle, you persuade, you entice and you probably end up compromising in some way. Business people are no different. So when these groups meet, people come into the room with their own objectives. They may be pushing for more power for their department. They may be desperate to convince others they know the right way forward. They may have a particular passion they want to pursue. They may be eager to take a few more risks, or play it safe. All these ideas and aspirations come into the melting pot, and out of this come the firm's objectives. The results, therefore, are usually a compromise between all the different groups – the owners, the different managers and the employees.

This is certainly the view of Cyert and March who developed the Behavioural Theory of the firm in 1963. Cyert and March see organisations as being formed around individuals and groups who combine to pursue their mutual interests. Their interests may not be completely shared, but the organisation is seen by all participants as the most effective way of achieving their individual goals. 'It may not be perfect but it may be the best we've got'.

Be SMART

For objectives to be effective they should have the following features:

- **S**pecific – it must be clear what you are focusing on, eg increasing profits or sales
- **M**easurable – all objectives should have a quantifiable element so that progress can be properly measured (eg a 20% increase)
- **A**greed – there is no point in simply telling someone what their target is; they may nod their head but they won't necessarily be committed to it because they haven't been involved in setting it. A target is more likely to be achieved if the people who have to hit it help to set it
- **R**ealistic – a target that will never be hit is not worth setting. It simply serves to devalue the whole process and loses the confidence and commitment of those involved
- **T**ime specific – it needs to be clear when an objective needs to be achieved, otherwise people may drag it out for years.

A good objective might be 'to increase profits by 10% in the next two years'. This is specific (profits), measurable (by 10%), time specific (two years); hopefully it is also agreed and realistic.

Setting objectives

The process of setting objectives should involve staff. Walking in one day and telling employees what they have to achieve is hardly likely to motivate them. It is much better to discuss the targets with the very people who know what is and what is not feasible. This does not mean the objectives should be easy – all targets should stretch people and make them feel that they have to make an effort to achieve them.

Managers at the drinks company Diageo talk of setting HATs – Hairy Audacious Targets – which are set high enough to make it a challenge to achieve them, but not too high to demotivate.

If set properly, objectives:

- should help bind people to the organisation – employees should be able to see what they are doing to help the business as a whole achieve its goals
- should motivate – an employee should have a clear idea of what will be regarded as a good piece of work

- should serve as a means of review – at appraisal meetings performance can be discussed relative to the target.

The use of objectives within an organisation can be made systematic using an approach that was called Management by Objectives (MBO) by Peter Drucker in his book *The Practice of Management* (1954). Using MBO, subordinates and superiors at every level agree on their targets, so everyone knows what they are supposed to do. Objectives are cascaded down. For example, the organisation may be trying to increase profits by 20%; this may require sales to increase by 30%. This may then require the brand manager of product A to boost A's sales by 35%. The sales manager for Europe for product A may therefore need to increase sales by 25% and this may require UK sales to increase by 20%, and so on. The overall objective is therefore broken down into more and more specific targets. If each person hits their targets, the business as a whole will achieve its goals.

The danger of such an approach is that it may lead to fixation! We become so obsessed by the objectives that this becomes our whole definition of success. As a result, we may ignore many interesting opportunities which rear their heads along the way, simply because they are not written down as part of our objectives.

Focusing on a limited number of objectives can also lead to unwelcome changes in behaviour. In December 2001, nine hospital trusts in the UK were found to be fiddling the figures just to hit their targets. To reduce the number of people on their waiting lists, for example, they secretly introduced a waiting list for the waiting list! They took patients off the 'main' list thereby hitting their target.

It is also very important to make sure the target set is the right one. One local council in the UK set targets for the percentage of rubbish collected which was recycleable. As a result, the waste removal companies asked a large number of households in the area to divide up their rubbish between recyclable and non-recycleable items. They hit their targets, even though when it came to disposing of the rubbish it was all lumped back together again. The target was for collecting recycleable rubbish, NOT for the proportion of rubbish actually recycled! If the target is wrong the behaviour will be as well.

Making the MOST of it

- The **M**ission describes the overall purpose of the organisation: 'to be the world's greatest football team'
- The **O**bjectives set out the precise targets the organisation wants to achieve: 'to win the league within two years'

- The **S**trategy is the long-term plan necessary to achieve the objectives: 'to play attacking football'
- The **T**actics are the way in which the strategy is to be implemented in the short term: 'to start training next week on improving our passing skills'.

Summary points

▶ an objective is a quantifiable target; it sets out what the firm wants to achieve

▶ objectives can unite and provide direction; employees can see where the organisation is heading

▶ profit is often the objective of private sector organisations – it provides rewards for the owners and is a source of finance for investment

▶ however, profit is not the only objective. Firms are also likely to have social, environmental and employee-based objectives

▶ a firm's objectives are likely to be a compromise between different groups within the firm

▶ objectives can distort behaviour; if you set the wrong targets, you will get the wrong type of behaviour

 **THINK about it!**

Identify three objectives that would be appropriate for you in your personal life, work or study for the next six months. How would your boss/personal tutor respond to these objectives? How might the objectives differ if they wrote them for you? Review your objectives in six months. Did you achieve them?

Business strategy

A firm's strategy is its long-term plan to achieve its objectives. It usually involves a significant commitment of resources, and once set into play it can be difficult to reverse. Therefore a strategic decision involves an opportunity cost.

A firm's strategy:
- sets out how it will compete and the markets in which it will compete
- aims to provide the businesss with an advantage over the competition
- must adapt to meet the changing requirements of the environment
- must achieve the objectives set for it by the organisation's stakeholders.

Strategic decisions are big, risky and involve major choices. They are not simply tinkering with price or costs, they involve a decision about the markets in which the firm will fight and the whole way in which it will compete. Not surprisingly then, strategic decisions are made at a senior level. They require an overview of the business as a whole and where it is headed. Will we win by competing at the top end of the market? Is it better to fight in a niche or in the mass market? Should we expand overseas?

Get the strategy wrong and success becomes difficult if not impossible, as Marconi discovered in the late 1990s when it moved from defence into telecom, at a time when the latter was collapsing. In 2001, Marconi declared losses of £5 bn. If, however, the strategy is right, you are in the right market at the right time with the right skills.

Success through innovation: Southwest Airlines and Ikea

The approach of the American airline Southwest Airlines is a good example of successful business strategy. When it was established, Southwest Airlines did not set out to run a better airline than existing firms such as American Airlines or United by offering greater punctuality or better-dressed attendants. Instead, it created a completely new kind of business. It flew from local airports and offered a cheap, no frills flight that the others did not. And instead of offering better food it offered no food at all! It flew only short haul, not long haul. To win, South West didn't mess around with competitors' models – it changed the rules entirely. Its strategy was innovative and tapped into a new niche. Easyjet adopted a very similar and equally successful strategy in Europe, eating into the profits of established carriers such as British Airways.

The furniture retailer Ikea also started out with a clear and, at the time, unique strategy, deciding from the outset that it would not serve people who wanted detailed advice and help. Instead, it offers cleanly designed products in vast, brightly lit warehouse stores at rock bottom prices. Customers have to retrieve the furniture from the shelves, transport them home and assemble them themselves. This is very different from many other furniture companies. Ikea staked out its territory and has fought there very successfully ever since.

Success through better value: Tesco

The UK retailer Tesco has become one of the world's leading retailers, with a market value of more than £17 bn and employing over 260,000 people in Asia, eastern Europe and Britain. Tesco's major successes came under the leadership of Terry Leahy. Leahy's success began in the 1990s when he was marketing director and took the unusual step of asking customers what they wanted! 'They told us we were spending too much time copying Sainsbury and not enough giving them what they needed'. In surveys and focus groups, customers said they wanted Tesco to go back to its roots as the 'pile it high sell it cheap' chain rather than try and move upmarket. 'We rediscovered value,' says Leahy, which led to the launch of the cheap and cheerful Value products.

City investors hated this strategy because they were convinced that Sainsbury's had the correct aim by moving up-market. The City was wrong – Tesco achieved a market share of over 22% compared to Sainsbury's 16% in 2001 (in 1995, Tesco had had just 12.4%). The overall strategy of investment of profits in improved services (a loyalty card that rewarded shoppers with money off vouchers, 24-hour store opening and home shopping via the internet) has been responsible for remarkable sales growth for Tesco. This has more than compensated for the decision by the company not to widen its operating profit margins.

Success by avoiding a head-on collision: PepsiCo

Another example of a highly successful strategy has been the radical restructuring of PepsiCo. Under the leadership of Mr Roger Enrico, Pepsi's restaurant and bottling businesses were sold off and the company focused once again on the two areas which had made it great in the first place: salty snacks and beverages. These changes were part of an overall strategy of moving away from head to head competition with Coca Cola. This was a big leap for a man forever associated with the cola wars of the 1980s when, after national taste tests, Pepsi-Cola pushed ahead of Coke in the US for the first time. Mr Enrico, Pepsi's boss even then, now dismisses himself as 'young and brash' at the time, especially given that he wrote a book that now seems slightly premature, called '*The Other Guy Blinked: How Pepsi Won the Cola Wars*'!

Pepsi's decision to get back to basics, plus an overhaul at Coca Cola, widened the gap between the two companies; PepsiCo concentrated on developing snacks while Coke became even more committed to becoming an all-beverage company. Central to this is a notion that with Frito-Lay, PepsiCo can play its snacks and soft drinks off against each other, a strategy called 'Power of One'. PepsiCo boasts that it is the largest source of sales for retailers such as Wal-Mart because it supplies both the snacks and the beverages. 'Just the simple things, such as putting the snacks across from the soft drinks, can increase sales by 3 to 4 per cent,' Mr Enrico says, 'The soft drinks bring the traffic in and the snacks give you the margin.'

This was the rationale that led Pepsi-Cola to merge with Frito-Lay, forming PepsiCo back in 1965. At the time, Don Kendall, chief executive of Pepsi-Cola, said, 'You make them thirsty and I'll give them something to drink.' Frito-Lay, which produces potato and corn chips, such as Doritos, now generates more than 60% of the revenues and profits for PepsiCo. Beverages are still a substantial part of the business but really only in North America, which accounts for nearly 24% of profits.

'The Power of One' was recognition that PepsiCo could not win the war – any war – on colas alone. Its soft-drink sales outside the US are less than a quarter of Coke's, and in some big markets, the company accepted it was unlikely to ever to beat its competitor. Instead, it has selected a few countries – India, China, Russia – where it has a better chance of winning the cola battle and has sought profits by competing in other product areas.

Summary points

▶ a strategy is a long-term plan to achieve a firm's objectives

▶ a strategy involves high levels of resources

▶ a strategy is highly risky

▶ strategies differ between organiations: success may come from focusing on certain key markets and activities, by developing an innovative service or by concentrating on the value provided. Most likely it comes from a combination of all of these!

THINK about it!

Think about the strategy of your own organisation or one you know well. Answer the questions below:

- Name of organisation:
- What markets does it compete in?
- How does it position itself relative to the competition? E.g. how does it try to attract customers/clients/students?
- Has its strategy changed in the past few years?
- How could it change its strategy in the future?

Types of strategy

Ansoff Matrix

The different types of strategy which an organisation pursues can be categorised using the Ansoff Matrix[2]. This examines a firm's strategy in terms of the products it offers and the markets in which it competes. It is illustrated below:

		Products	
		existing	*new*
Markets	*existing*	market penetration	product development
	new	market development	diversification

Market penetration is likely to be the safest of these strategies. A firm stays secure in its existing markets offering existing products. It has knowledge and experience of these areas and therefore is minimising its risk. Diversification, by comparison, involves new products and markets, and therefore is likely to involve much more uncertainty. Market penetration involves changes to the existing marketing, eg new prices, new packaging or more promotional activities that increase sales of the current product range. It may be achieved by encouraging brand switching, attracting new users to the product or increasing the product usage (eg a simple instruction to 'shampoo your hair twice with this product to get the best results' can double the usage).

Market development, by comparison, involves a greater risk in that the demands of the new segment or new region may differ from the markets you are used to. For example, an airline may expand into new routes and find that the regulations, administration and expectations of customers are different. Simply because one product or concept works in one country does not mean it will necessarily work in another, as several UK retailers have found to their cost in continental Europe and the USA.

The third option, **product development**, involves developing new products. The majority of these will fail (only about one in five new products survive), so this approach certainly requires nerve. However, some companies such as 3M remain committed to product development as a means of competing in their markets. 3M's stated objective is to generate 30% of its sales from products developed within the past four years. Similarly, Canon recently ran an advertising campaign highlighting that it takes out five patents each day – innovation clearly counts in this business.

If you do decide that you are going to pursue product development, evidence suggests that the chances of success are higher for firms which make minor developments to a product (such as new features or new models) rather than focusing on breakthrough technology. Radical innovations (such as DVD) can be highly profitable, but tend to be riskier and take longer to establish themselves and prove their value to consumers. Sony had a well-known and expensive failure with its Betamax video technology which lost out to VHS. However, even the success of VHS shows the danger of innovation – it was developed by Philips but more successfully exploited by other firms such as Matsushita. On the other hand, ignoring product development is also dangerous – if you are not careful, developments in technology by others may wipe you out. Just look at the threat to the traditional music industry from the internet, or to traditional films from digital cameras.

The fourth strategy, **diversification**, definitely requires nerves of steel – to be willing and able to move into such new areas is a major challenge. However, it can be done with great success: witness Nintendo's move into consumer electronics from playing cards, and Nokia's move from paper into mobile phones (via various other industries).

Other types of strategy

Apart from the Ansoff Matrix, strategies can also be categorised in terms of what the firm is trying to achieve. For example:

■ **Stability**: this occurs when firms basically 'go with the flow'. For example, if the market grows, so does the business, but the managers do not actively seek to outperform the market – they keep their heads down. This approach can work if the market is fairly secure, allowing the business to focus on improving its efficiency (and therefore profits) while not being threatened by external change.

- **Growth**: this strategy is adopted by organisations that believe they are strong and ready to expand. It suits managers who want to take risks and are eager to grow.
- **Retrenchment**: this strategy involves withdrawing from a market or sector. This may be because demand is falling or because key people or skills have been lost making it undesirable to stay in this market. Boots expanded heavily overseas, but in 2002 announced its withdrawal from many of these markets. Marks and Spencer pulled out of overseas operations in 2001.

How to compete: low cost v differentiation (Porter)

As well as deciding whether to expand, and if so into which type of markets, a firm must also decide on how it is going to compete. Using Michael Porter's analysis[3] we can describe two main approaches to competing: cost leadership and differentiation.

A cost leadership strategy aims to provide similar benefits to the competition but at a lower price. Think of Aldi and Asda. A differentiation strategy aims to provide more benefits than the competition which can justify a higher price. Think of Savile Row suits, Rolls Royce cars and Thornton's chocolates. Both of these are ways of adding value for the customer and winning their business and their loyalty. One focuses on offering a lower price; the other focuses on more benefits. (Obviously if you can do both you're on to a good thing!) The worst situation is when you are offering similar goods and services to competitors but at a higher price – no one will willingly buy from you.

Let's say you are entering the hotel business, for example. You might offer accommodation similar to other firms, but try to undercut the other providers on price. To do this you might try and reduce overheads (eg offer a very basic service, not including breakfast or dinner), or you might try to bargain harder than everyone else with your suppliers or staff to get better rates; alternatively you might deliberately set up in low cost locations. However, the question you must ask yourself before starting in this type of business, is whether you can really establish a cost advantage, and if so can you sustain it? Can you really get costs lower than the competition? Do you have a sustainable advantage? If not, you may not be able to compete for very long.

Alternatively, you may differentiate your offerings by providing unusual facilities – a swimming pool, a golf course, a superb restaurant or excellent locations. If you can sufficiently differentiate what you offer, you may be able to charge more than the competition but still provide better value for money.

The question again is whether this is sustainable – do you have a combination of people, resources, contacts and offerings that cannot easily be imitated? If they can be imitated, you may find profits are soon eroded. In 1989 HSBC managed to differentiate itself in the highly competitive banking world with the launch of First Direct, which bypassed the traditional channels of bank branches and provided free phone banking. At the time it represented a revolution in banking, but has since been widely imitated and then rivalled by the growth of internet banking. Its early success highlights the value of differentiation but the story since then shows the difficulty of sustaining an advantage over time.

Summary points

▶ Ansoff identifies four strategies: market development, market penetration, new product development and diversification

▶ some strategies are riskier than others – nerves of steel may be needed to diversify!

▶ Michael Porter highlights the difference between low cost and differentiation strategies; this shows how firms can compete in very different ways in the same market

Do you think it is possible to be both a 'differentiated' and 'low cost' provider? Can you think of examples of firms who have achieved this? What problems might there be combining the two strategies?

Where do strategies come from?

This will vary from organisation to organisation. In some there will be a senior management group, clearly responsible for strategic thinking. The plan will be developed formally and rolled out to the various divisions and departments. The planning horizon may be five to ten years, and the process a very systematic and logical one. In the words of the great writer on strategy, Igor Ansoff, 'Strategic management is a comprehensive procedure which starts with a strategic diagnosis and guides the firm through a series of additional steps which culminate in new products, markets and technologies'.

However, in other organisations strategic planning is less formal, less clear cut and more ad hoc. Rather than laying out a clear plan of action, some firms react to what is happening around them or gradually watch as a strategy emerges over time. They take action and gradually over time it becomes clear which strategy they are adopting!

While Ansoff's approach – which stresses a scientific and highly logical approach – has a certain beauty, putting it into practice can be very difficult, not least because the world does not always develop in the way you expected. Furthermore, strategic planning can be time-consuming and can actually harm the firm if the strategy turns out to be out of date. Some commentators believe strategic planning is often inappropriate. Henry Mintzberg in *The Rise and Fall of Strategic Planning* (1994)[4] writes: 'too much analysis gets in our way'. Jack Welch, at the hugely successful American conglomerate General Electric, dispensed with all the strategic planning and set a simple goal, 'Be number one or two in an industry or else get out'. He believed that if the vision was clear, managers could work out for themselves how to get there.

Success by accident, not design: Honda and the USA

In 1975 the UK government published a report prepared by Boston Consulting Group (BCG) on various strategies open to the British motorcycle industry. It stated that, 'As recently as 1960 only four per cent of the Japanese motorcycle production was exported. By this time however, the Japanese had developed huge production volumes in small motorcycles in their domestic markets and volume-related cost reductions had followed. This resulted in a highly competitive cost position which the Japanese used as a springboard for penetration of world markets with small motorcycles in the early 1960s'. This report therefore suggested that Honda deliberately built a commanding cost advantage and then specifically targeted the bottom end of the US market (especially with its lightweight 50cc Supercub bike) to exploit this advantage. This looked like a superb example of strategic planning – Honda had carefully identified what they wanted to achieve and how they were going to do it, and then executed the plan brilliantly.

However, this may not be the real story. In 1982 Richard Pascale, a professor at Stanford, flew to Japan and interviewed the six Japanese executives responsible for Honda's entry into the market in 1959. These managers gave a very different account of the Honda experience. According to Pascale the low price of the Honda was due to the design of its engine and not due to economies of scale. In fact, production at Honda was quite inefficient. Furthermore, Honda did not deliberately aim to dominate the market with smaller machines at all. When it began to sell in America, it was offering bigger bikes. Success came by accident. Honda assumed the little bikes would not be suitable for a market where everything seemed to be bigger and more luxurious. However, the managers used the small Supercubs to get around the cities themselves and this generated interest. Eventually sales took off and Honda achieved a breakthrough into the market.

The Honda experience highlights that strategy need not always be formulated in advance – it sometimes emerges along the way. This is called the emergent strategy. The realised strategy of any firm is likely to be a combination of the deliberate and the emergent strategies.

If it goes wrong: change!

Connolly is one of the most famous names in the leather industry, even though its sales have never exceeded £45 m. Founded in 1878, it sells leather for some of the most expensive car seats such as Aston Martin, Rolls Royce and Jaguar. However, the company made operating losses throughout the 1990s, and in 1996 Connolly made a dramatic strategic move by entering the mass market via a joint venture in the US. It identified a problem and changed its strategy from niche to mass, producing fewer exclusive seats for a range of firms. Its sales soon grew but the company continued to be unprofitable; it bit the bullet and sold the US venture. Once again it was time to change! This time it focused on its UK operations and decided to close its old tanning operations at Canterbury and inefficient cutting facilities in Wimbledon, and move to Ashford, Kent. Its new business plan focused once again on the top end niche of the market such as Bentley and Rolls Royce. Its target was about 4,500 hides a week, not the 11,500 it processed in 2000, and it focused on more expensive hides. 'We will be smaller but everything will be under control. Bigger is not necessarily better,' according to a consultant hired by the firm to turn it around. The future of Connolly may still be doubtful but the company has shown its willingness to change its strategy to survive.

Reasons for strategic change include new managers with new ideas, and new opportunities created by market change. Umbro has been making football equipment for over 70 years. In 1999, new owners of the company looked to develop a different strategy exploiting the opportunity the internet provides. The vision is to make the company 'the authority' on football by establishing umbro.com. This website was seen as a way of connecting with potential and existing younger customers. Visit it and see what you think.

Summary points

▶ the planned strategy is what you expected to happen

▶ the realised strategy is what actually happens

▶ strategies may be scientifically planned, or they may occur more randomly

▶ strategies can be changed – you don't have to keep doing the same thing!

You are the manager of a football team. Your objective is to make sure you are not relegated this season. Identify one strategy you might adopt to achieve this objective. Identify one reason why you might have chosen this strategy. Identify one factor which might cause you to change your strategy half way through the season.

Leave it to me; I'll manage!

What is management?

Effective management lies at the heart of a successful organisation. It involves setting out the direction of the business, coordinating the actions of different people and their teams, picking people up when they are down and getting them focused once again. It involves understanding the key issues in a problem and knowing what does and what does not matter. Bad managers fail to inspire, fail to get their work done on time and do not make the right decisions. Good managers cut through the detail to the most significant issues and get them right.

According to Naylor[5], 'Management is the process of achieving organisational objectives within a changing environment by balancing efficiency, effectiveness and equity, obtaining the most from limited resources and working with and through other people.' This definition includes many important aspects of the management process. Firstly, it recognises that managers are there to achieve the objectives of the organisation rather than their own. They are not there for their own glory (at least they are not supposed to be); they are there to fulfil the wishes of their owners. Secondly, it highlights the changing nature of the business world. A good manager must be flexible because the problems he or she is likely to face will change over time. Picture a juggler with 'crisis', 'disaster', 'opportunity', 'threat' written on the balls he is juggling, and you are getting the idea.

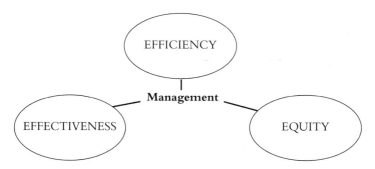

Naylor's definition also indicates three areas in which managers may be assessed. **Efficiency** measures how well the organisation's resources are transformed into outputs. **Effectiveness** is whether the managers are doing the right thing – how far a stated objective is achieved. These two may not be the same. In order to get the job done, it may need investment in resources which could be inefficient. The last criteria is **equity**, which involves the distribution of outputs among recipients, ie, who benefits from the results – for example, to what extent should the rewards go to the owners compared to the employees? Too much to the owners, and the employees may not perform effectively; too much to the employees, and the managers may be ousted by the owners.

Management is not a solitary process. It usually involves utilising other people within the organisation effectively. Indeed, Mary Parket Follett[6] defined management as the process of 'getting things done through others'. These 'things' must help the firm face both present and future challenges. They have to cope with the day-to-day demands of running an organisation – the demands from staff and the inevitable crises. Managers must also look ahead to ensure the organisation changes in line with its environment and opportunities.

What makes a good manager?

In his study of leadership, Warren Bennis[7], professor at the University of Southern California, argues that good managers have seven distinct skills. Almost all senior managers have three – technical competence, the faculty for abstract thought and a record that commands respect – but only the very best combine these with

- taste – the ability to identify and cultivate talent
- judgement – the knack of making difficult decisions in a short time-frame with imperfect data
- people skills – the ability to communicate, motivate and delegate
- character – integrity, drive, optimism, curiosity and courage.

These 'soft' skills are most important in times of economic crisis. At times like these, taste is required to avoid losing the company's best talent as part of restructuring or delayering; judgement is needed to hammer out a plan quickly; people skills determine whether those who survive the restructuring remain motivated and character is needed to drive the change through.

What do managers really do?

Ask some employees and they'll probably tell you that their managers do nothing but drink coffee all day and chat. Read most textbooks, however, and you would think that managers are the most logical, calculating individuals that have ever existed. Apparently they sit behind their well-polished mahogany desks in their large offices looking out from the tenth floor onto the business below them. There they sit in isolation, rarely interrupted, spending their day thinking strategically. They plan, they forecast, they move their troops around their empires. The managers' offices are like the war rooms in the old films; managers receive information from the front and gently push troops around the board.

In reality most managers' days are filled with conversations and meetings. They are often fire-fighting – fixing the latest problem, solving the latest crisis, handling the latest dilemma. They tend to get little time – certainly not as long as they would like – to plan strategically. In fact, strategies often emerge rather than being planned in some darkened room and then unleashed on the world. Mintzberg found in his studies that successful senior managers were not 'reflective strategists'; instead they tended to be people who had to act intuitively. They relied as much on information and anecdotes as hard data and analysis. They spent a lot of their time talking and meeting and much less time reading and writing.

Management is not necessarily for the long-term planner, the chess player thinking ten moves ahead; more often than not, it is for the street fighter reacting to each assault.

Obviously, the precise tasks of managers will differ according to the level they are at in the organisation. The higher up they are, the more strategic they tend to be and the less concerned they will be with the day-to-day affairs. Nevertheless, all managers tend to undertake the following functions that were first identified by Henri Fayol[8] in the early 1900s:
- *planning* what the firm needs to be doing and where it needs to be going
- *organising* the various resources needed to succeed
- *coordinating* these resources so that they interlink effectively
- *controlling* the activities to ensure they are on target.

At the same time managers play various roles within the firm. According to Henry Mintzberg[9] these can be analysed under three headings:

- interpersonal roles – these include acting as a figurehead of the organisation, motivating subordinates and liaising with outside groups
- informational roles – these include collecting and giving out information and acting as a spokesperson
- decisional roles – deciding how to allocate resources, reward people, handle disturbances and negotiate.

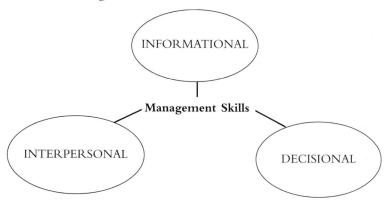

Summary points

- managers decide on how to allocate resources

- management is about managing people and 'getting things done through others'

- management involves managing the present and planning for the future; it is a continuous and dynamic process

- Fayol identified the key aspects of management as planning, organising, coordinating and controlling

- Mintzberg identifies three key roles of management: interpersonal, informational and decisional

THINK about it!

Identify three features in your personality which you think would make you a good manager. Try to think of a situation where you demonstrated each of the qualities you have identified.

How should you manage?

Given the importance of effective management to business success, it's not surprising that a lot of work has been done to identify the best way of managing or the best person to be a manager. The initial research looked for particular traits which could define a successful manager. For example, are good managers always extrovert, ambitious, confident or socialisers? Unfortunately, findings from such studies have proved inconclusive – the qualities of a good leader do not seem easy to define.

A second type of study has focused on the way in which people are managed – this tried to isolate whether there is one style of management which is most appropriate. Generally, commentators have distinguished between the autocratic/authoritarian approach (where people are told what to do) and the democratic approach (where managers listen to what subordinates have to say and involve them in decision making). Of course it is a question of degree – it is not that a manager is completely authoritarian or completely democratic. It is simply a question of whether the style they adopt is generally more one than the other, and to what extent they exhibit such characteristics.

These styles have been seen to have varying success according to factors such as the circumstances, the nature of the manager, the employees and the task. The right style when dealing with an emergency and a team of untrained, inexperienced staff is likely to be very different from the right style when you have plenty of time, you are looking for a high level of creativity and your staff are able and highly competent. This led to the growth of the contingency approach that argued that the most effective type of management would be contingent on a range of factors. According to Fiedler's study[10], therefore, the manager has to be changed to match the situation. Key factors in determining the 'best' style included the clarity of the task and the manager's relations with her subordinates.

It seems then that there may be no such thing as a perfect manager or a perfect style. The style will need to vary depending on the circumstances.

Leadership v management

Is a leader different from a manager? Perhaps the important difference between a leader and a manager is that the former is looking further ahead; you may be able to *manage* the here and now, but leaders take us onwards into new battles.

According to Warren Bennis[11], 'leaders conquer the context – the volatile, turbulent ambiguous surroundings that sometimes seem to conspire against us and will surely suffocate us if we let them – while managers surrender to it'. He highlights the difference between managers and leaders in his eyes:

- the manager administers; the leader innovates
- the manager is a copy; the leader is an original
- the manager maintains; the leader develops
- the manager relies on control; the leader inspires trust
- the manager has his eye on the bottom line; the leader has his eye on the horizon
- the manager does things right; the leader does the right thing.

So what's the big deal about management?

There are probably very few things you will ever read in a management book that either you do not know or that are not fairly obvious. However, there is a huge difference between the theory and the practice. Building a team, taking the long-term view, inspiring them with your vision, and leading them through the trials and tribulations of any project only takes a few lines on paper, but in reality can be hours of negotiation, argument, discussion. In many cases it leads to failure. Not everyone can lead, get a team on board and ready to follow them. So do spare a thought for the realities of management – for the difficulties of dealing with people (and their personal ambitions, career aspirations, anxieties, fears and angers) and for the difficulties of managing within a budget, of balancing lots of conflicting aims and of having to deal with the unavoidable and unexpected. It's not all easy!

Summary points

- the most appropriate style of management may depend on factors such as the clarity of the task and the manager's relations with his or her subordinates

- managers are often interrupted and have little free time

- managers are often 'fire fighters' rather than planners; they have to react to crises

- leaders may be different from managers: according to Mintzberg, 'the manager does things right; the leader does the right thing'

Leadership in action: Jack Welch and General Electric

One of the greatest business leaders of the last fifty years is undoubtedly Jack Welch. As Chief Executive of General Electric (GE), Jack built one of the largest and most successful companies in the world, worth over $500 bn, operating in more than 100 countries and employing over 310,000 people worldwide. The company sells everything from light bulbs and dishwashers to aero engines and financial services, and has revenues of over $110 bn a year. Year after year the company and Jack Welch have won awards for being the most admired company or business leader.

The road to success

Welch built this success by a remarkable hands-on approach – despite the amazing size of General Electric, Welch's presence was everywhere. Welch joined the company in 1960 and rapidly worked his way up. According to Jay Conger, professor of leadership at the London Business School, one of Welch's strengths was the ability to identify new trends and then rebuild the business. 'Control your destiny or die' was one of Welch's favourite sayings, demonstrating his view that companies make their own success. Welch insisted that every GE business was number one or number two in any market in which it competed. If it could not achieve this, he insisted the firm left that market.

Welch also insisted on 'speed, simplicity, self-confidence'. When he first took over General Electric he set out to smash up the bureaucracy. He fired thousands of employees and removed several layers of management, acquiring the nickname 'Neutron Jack' along the way. Within five years of being appointed Chief Executive he had cut 118,000 jobs (about 25% of the workforce). 'I hated it and it hurt. But I hated bureaucracy and waste even more,' said Welch. Welch was continually reshaping General Electric as opportunities arose. Under him the company undertook over 1,700 acquisitions; he also made numerous disposals when he felt the businesses could not be market leaders.

Despite a reputation for being tough, Welch says he was not tough enough: 'The lesson I have learned consistently over the years is that I have been in many cases too cautious. I should have torn down the structures sooner, sold off weak businesses faster than I did. Almost everything should and could have been done faster. This so-called "Toughest Boss in America" wasn't tough enough!'

There is no doubt that despite his critics Welch's managerial style inspired and invigorated people within the organisation. He insisted on getting the right people in the right places and ensuring the best ideas flowed through the organisation to maximise its performance. Welch demanded much and got it from many employees, who responded to his call that 'If it bothers you, yell at it, scream at it, break it!'

He built the company and its culture around himself, and put his own values at the very core of the organisation. These values are formally declared in a Management Values statement which states that GE leaders:

- always act with unyielding integrity
- are passionately focused on driving customer success
- live quality ... ensure that the customer is always its first beneficiary ... and use it to accelerate growth
- insist on excellence and are intolerant of bureaucracy
- act in a boundaryless fashion ... always search for and apply the best ideas, regardless of their source
- prize global intellectual capital and the people that provide it ... build diverse teams to maximize it
- see change for the growth opportunities it brings ... ie 'digitization'
- create a clear, simple, customer-centered vision ... and continually renew and refresh its execution
- create an environment of 'stretch', excitement, informality and trust ... reward improvements ... and celebrate results
- demonstrate ... always with infectious enthusiasm for the customer ... the '4-E's' of GE leadership: the personal **E**nergy to welcome and deal with the speed of change ... the ability to create an atmosphere that **E**nergizes others ... the **E**dge to make difficult decisions ... and the ability to consistently **E**xecute.

Summary points

▶ Jack Welch is a corporate hero

▶ read his book[12]

Jack Welch was clearly a unique individual and highly successful manager. Do you think such people are born as leaders, or can you train people to become great managers?

What is culture?

When you first walk into a business it does not take long to get a feel for the place. The way people are dressed, the way they talk to each other and the way the place is decorated all give clues about what the people here think is important. It may feel modern and dynamic, or traditional and stodgy. When you actually start working at a firm it soon becomes even clearer what is the accepted way of working – the way they do things, what is and is not acceptable behaviour, the people who are admired, revered and praised, what you can and can't get away with. You will also get to know the corporate rituals – the morning gathering around the coffee machine, the Friday lunchtime visit to the pub, the annual Christmas party.

Values, attitudes, principles

All of these things depend on the **culture** of the organisation – the values attitudes and beliefs of the employees who work in the firm. By 'values' we mean the fundamental principles that people hold regarding what is right or wrong, important and unimportant; eg, do we value being honest with our customers if we cannot help them? how important is it to work as a team? Your values naturally determine your attitudes; if you value innovation then your attitude to a proposal to invest in research and development is likely to be favourable.

Some organisations have very clear values and attitudes. For example, at Wal-Mart, Sam Walton the founder insisted that the customer comes first. All associates (as Wal-Mart employees are called) must 'promise that whenever you come within 10 feet of a customer you will look him in the eye, greet him and ask him if you can help him'. They must also obey the SUNDOWN rule, by which employees should answer customers' requests by sundown of the day they are received.

Culture is an incredibly powerful thing. It affects the way people think and the way they behave, which in turn affects the success of the business. But as well as helping firms to succeed, culture can also be destructive. In 2002, Enron became the world's largest corporate bankruptcy when it was discovered that many of its so-called profits did not actually exist. Part of the reason for the firm's problems was said to be the never-ending demand for higher profits by the directors. Under enormous pressure to produce results, managers looked for any way of boosting their profits, even if this meant inventing them! When the errors in the accounts were discovered, Enron went almost overnight from being the seventh largest company with £43 bn worth of assets on its books, to being bankrupt when the debts were discovered.

The importance of the organisational culture to the success of a firm can be seen in experience of Cisco, a company which produces computer hardware. Under Chief Executive, John Chambers, the Cisco organisation rose from less than 3000 employees to more than 44,000 in just six years. This represents extraordinary growth. But in doing so, the firm lost some of the entrepreneurial spirit and creativity that propelled it to the top ranks of global technology elite. In order to control such growth some argued that it become too bureaucratic, turning off the very people the firm wanted to attract. It became the giant when what it wanted to do was attract people who wanted to work for the small rebel business. To try and avoid some of these problems, Chambers deliberately set out to acquire dozens of small cutting edge companies in networking technology as it grew. Even so, commentators claim it has lost it ability to encourage 'out of the box' thinking.

Regional and national culture

The behaviour of employees will be affected by regional and national cultures as well as the organisational culture. Travel around the world and you soon see differences in peoples' attitudes to education, religion, work, the family, the law and so on. This all affects how employees need to be managed, what they regard as acceptable behaviour and what expectations and values they have. Ignore a nation's culture and you are likely to struggle to understand how to manage a business there or market your products effectively.

Summary points

▶ culture varies from one organisation to another; these differences can be measured in several ways, including the attitude to risk and teamwork

▶ there's no such thing as the 'right' culture; what matters is whether the culture is right for the business circumstances

 **THINK about it!**

Think about the organisation where you study or work. Describe its culture in ten lines or less below.

Culture in action

Hewlett Packard

The importance of culture can be seen in the success of Hewlett Packard (HP) in its early years. The business was established in the late 1930s in Palo Alto, California and its culture was the result of strong beliefs of founders Bill Hewlett and Dave Packard. Bill and Dave, as they were known in the company, created a formal statement of HP's basic values, which included serving everyone who had a stake in the company with integrity and fairness, including customers, suppliers, employees, shareholders and society in general. They helped to build the culture by hiring like-minded people and letting their values guide their actions. For example, they made it clear HP was not a 'hire and fire company' even when times were tough. They pioneered what they called 'management by walking around' (MBWA), stressing the need for managers to be visible, to be talking to staff and to be listening.

Unlike most other firms at the time, Dave and Bill built open-plan offices, encouraged employees to use their budgets to pursue their own passions and had regular Friday 'beer busts', when everyone got together to discuss how the week had gone over a beer. The HP Way involved (and to some still involves) values such as loving the product, loving the customer, being obsessed with innovation and quality, open communication, commitment to people, trust, confidence, informality, teamwork, sharing openness and autonomy.

United Parcels Service

Another organisation with a very strong organisational culture is UPS (United Parcel Service of America). UPS encourages employee ownership and has a strong belief in employees working their way up the organisation. Just look at the text of this UPS advert:

'Around here, our skin may be different colours but our blood is all the same. Brown. In other words, it's not where you're from or what you look like, it's how much you care. How good you are at your job. Just ask Hugo Paredes. Since starting out as a package unloader, he's been promoted five times. Today's he's a district manager with responsibility for 3,800 people, thousands of customers and millions of dollars of business. That's the way it works here. Everyone at UPS has the same opportunity for advancement as the next person. One might become a supervisor. One might become a district manager. One might even become chairman of the board'.

UK accounting firms – five very distinct cultures

You might think that an accountant is an accountant is an accountant. But you would be wrong. In the early 2000s, UK accounting was dominated by the Big Five: Andersen, Price Waterhouse Coopers, KPMG, Deloitte & Touche and Ernst and Young. Each of these had a distinct culture which affected
■ the way they dealt with clients (and the type of clients they attracted)
■ the type of employee they appealed to.

Andersen was well known as a highly demanding employer. If you worked for this company, you were taught to follow orders and do things the Andersen way. Senior staff were trained at the company's headquarters in Houston and then sent out to follow the Andersen way. KMPG by comparison, was known as a more youthful business. As the *Sunday Times* once said, 'If an accountant could ever be trendy he would work at KMPG'. The average age at KMPG was just 28. Ernst and Young was seen as being a much more serious place to work, attracting the sensible intellectuals.

So while we have five giant companies battling for world domination, employing in all cases over 80,000 people and in some cases well over 100,000, they are very distinctive and have their own personality. These different cultures naturally affect the way they do business and who they do business with.

Interestingly, Andersen made a major move to try and change its culture in the late 1990s by removing its dress code. Managers decided that because everyone turned up to work in 'company dress' (eg suits and ties) this sent out the message they all thought in the same way. Also, the mere fact that a dress code existed suggested that staff could not be trusted to decide for themselves what to wear. To reflect the stated desire for individual thinking and personal initiative, and to show how much employees' judgement was valued and trusted, employees were told they could wear what they want to work.

Summary points

> an organisation's culture can have a huge impact on its success

> the culture of organisations is as diverse and fascinating as the different cultures of the world

> there is no such thing as a 'right' or 'wrong' culture – just different cultures

THINK about it!

On page 60 you wrote about the culture of your existing organisation. How do you think this affects your performance as someone who works or studies there?

How does this organisation's culture differ from anywhere else you have worked or studied? In what ways is it better or worse?

Analysing culture and culture change

Handy's model

Handy[13] identifies four types of organisational culture in his famous model: web culture, role culture, task culture and people culture.

Web culture

This tends to occur in small entrepreneurial organisations where the founder or boss makes most of the decisions. Other individuals working in the organisation have some freedom to make decisions, but ultimately check back with the boss character. I recently worked in a business where everyone worked in one office except for the boss, who sat in his glass-panelled room looking out on everyone else. Every now and then he would come out, look at what everyone was doing and then tell them to change it. Nothing got done until it was cleared with him. This type of firm can often act quickly and react to market opportunities, but is heavily reliant on one or two people. Take away the boss and no one is used to taking responsibility for anything. This approach acts as a limitation to the firm's size – it cannot become too big because the central character cannot cope with the workload.

Role culture

This is a very common form of organisation in which rules and procedures are regarded as very important. Individuals tend to work within their own departments, and someone's power depends on their position in the hierarchy. Systems and set ways of doing things matter, as do job titles. As you work your way up you get a better title and probably more benefits to go with it (a bigger office to work in?). If anyone lower down wants to get anything done, the request must work its way up the hierarchy. This can be a very slow process and serves to keep the different elements of the business apart. Communication is vertical in this organisation; procedures have to be followed and this may limit innovation.

The task culture

This occurs in an organisation that creates teams to solve particular problems. People are selected on the basis of whether they can contribute to solving the particular problem in hand. The age or formal title of a person is less important than their expertise. This is quite a dynamic culture, focused on problem-solving.

People culture

This is a culture where people matter more than the organisation. It often occurs in doctors' practices or legal practices where the individuals see themselves as professionals working individually, rather than as part of a larger organisation. The ability to work independently is important in such cultures.

To identify which culture operates within a firm or even within a part of a firm (because cultures can differ between departments and between locations within the same firm), Charles Handy suggests a basic test. He suggests that if you ask someone what they do for a living the answer can be very revealing:

- 'I work for X (a person)' suggests a power culture – individuals identify with the boss and see what they do as revolving around him or her.
- 'I'm a … manager with XYZ Ltd' shows that they identify with the organisation; this is more likely to be a role culture.

- 'I'm with XYZ Ltd and working on the Z project' shows that the person identifies with the task in hand, and suggests a task culture.
- 'I am an accountant' suggests a person culture where people are what they do rather than who they work for.

Robbins' cultural differences

Culture can obviously be analysed in many different ways. As well as Handy's model, another well-known method of discussing corporate culture was developed by Robbins[14]. He highlights a number of distinct areas in which cultures may differ between organisations. For example:

- individual initiative – the degree of responsibility, freedom and independence that is encouraged within a firm
- risk tolerance – the degree to which employees are encouraged to be aggressive, innovative and risk taking
- direction – the degree to which an organisation creates clear objectives and peformance expectations
- integration – the degree to which units within the organisation are encouraged to operate in a coordinated manner
- control – the degree of rules and regulations, amount of supervision that is used to oversee and control employee behaviour
- conflict tolerance – the degree to which employees are encouraged to air conflicts and criticisms openly.

Changing the culture

This is where the problems really begin. Changing culture can be critical to a firm's success – raising the focus on quality, highlighting the importance of customer service, and stressing the need for teamwork are all key issues which may well need greater emphasis. How many times have you walked into a shop only to feel unwelcome? What about an office where watching the clock until finishing time seems more important than getting the job done?

But changing this type of behaviour can be difficult. People resent any suggestion that the way they do something is wrong. Or they may not agree with the managers' values about what really matters. By suggesting a different culture is needed, you are directly attacking the existing values. Culture change may come through reasoned argument – we can see that our existing line of thought was incorrect. You may start the change with education, explaining why the change is needed. However, it may take more than mere words or effective communication to win people over. You may need more direct ways of changing behaviour. Change the behaviour and the attitudes will follow, some say. But how can we do this? One way is to build a reward scheme that favours the new behaviours – if you think teamwork is important then provide team bonuses, not individual rewards.

If this carrot approach does not work, you could switch to the stick and force people to change, threatening that it will reduce their chances of promotion if they don't do things differently.

Summary points

- Handy identifies four typical cultures: web, role, task and people
- changing culture can be tough and unpopular
- to change culture you may inform or coerce (or both)

You have recently been promoted to manage a pub. The general culture there is poor. Customer service is not seen as particularly important, punctuality and attendance is poor and there is a general lack of interest among staff in the pub's success. One of your management colleagues has suggested you make an example of one of the staff early on, by being extremely tough with them and if necessary dismissing them, to set the tone. Do you think this is the right approach?

Culture change at Cadbury: focusing on value

In spring 1997, the Chief Executive of Cadbury Schweppes, John Sutherland, introduced a programme known as 'Managing for Value' (MFV). The aim was to bring about a significant change in the culture of the company. At the heart of this cultural change lay the concept of 'adding value' – to what extent were different activities within the firm really benefiting the owners? Instead of just assuming what they were doing was appropriate (after all, the company was profitable), managers were forced to examine the returns they were generating in relation to the opportunity costs of the funds being used. A 12% return may sound acceptable, but is not so impressive if the funds used to invest could have been earning 14%.

The consequence of the Managing for Value approach was that management became much more aware of the concept of opportunity costs, much more financially conscious and more thorough in its assessment of projects. Since it was first introduced, MFV has underpinned all of the company's actions. 'It is the most comprehensive and group-wide commitment to strategic change and management processes ever undertaken in Cadbury Schweppes' according to John Sutherland. *The Sunday Times* has described it simply as a 'management revolution'.

At the centre of the MFV programme are the company's corporate objectives. Sunderland has set out three clear financial targets:
- to achieve double-digit earnings growth annually
- to generate free cash flow of over £150 m a year
- to double total shareowner value within a four year time-scale.

To ensure this change is deep-rooted in the corporate culture, the remuneration and appraisal systems have been amended to reward good performance in these areas. This highlights an important aspect of cultural change – you cannot simply force it through, you have to provide real incentives to make people want to change their behaviour. There has also been an extensive programme of training and communication to explain why this type of change is regarded as necessary, what it actually entails and how staff will benefit. Over 4000 employees have so far undergone training in the MFV system.

In the past, Cadbury's had something of a paternalistic feel to it; MFV now imposes a real sense of accountability – managers are clearly assessed on their ability to generate value in their own areas of responsibility. This degree of accountability and a quantifiable method of assessment can be extremely liberating for managers. However, it also brings with it the pressure to perform and consequently can be met with some resistance when first introduced.

For some, MFV can prove too demanding; interestingly, within 18 months of MFV being introduced, half of the company's 150 senior managers were in different jobs. Managers that remain must demonstrate the 3 As: they must be adaptable, accountable and aggressive.

MFV has brought about a dramatic change in Cadbury's strategy. In the early 1990s, it set itself the goal of being a major global player in the non-cola drinks market. However, in the last few years it has been busy selling off these businesses in many of its overseas markets, generating over £1.5 bn in cash – a major strategic U-turn some say; a slight shift in ground says the company! Because of problems distributing its products Cadbury's decided its non-cola businesses would have more value for organisations that have a more extensive distribution network. It made more sense for Cadbury to focus its own efforts elsewhere.

The concept of added value (or economic value added, as it is sometimes called) is now seen by many analysts as an important measure of any firm's performance. In the past, it is claimed, far too much emphasis has been placed on a firm's return on capital employed without considering the cost of the funds used.

Summary points

▶ John Sutherland introduced a whole new approach at Cadbury to focus on value

▶ some of his managers were able to make this journey with him, while others were not and left the business

▶ Sutherland's new programme changed the way that managers viewed their business and made decisions; a change in culture involves a change in behaviour

THINK about it!

Sutherland's approach at Cadbury highlighted the importance of opportunity costs, ie finding out what else could be done with any money invested in a project. Imagine you have inherited £50,000 on the condition that you do not spend it for five years. Identify three options of what you could do with this money. Outline the case for and against each one. Which one of the three do you think you would choose? Why?

References

1. Gerry Johnson and Kevan Scholes *Exploring Corporate Strategy* 6th Edition (Financial Times Prentice Hall, 2002)
2. Igor Ansoff *Corporate Strategy* (McGraw Hill, 1965)
3. Michael Porter *Competitive Advantage* (Simon & Schuster 1995)
4. Henry Mintzberg *The Rise and Fall of Strategic Planning* (Financial Times Prentice Hall, 2000)
5. John Naylor *Management* (Financial Times Prentice Hall, 1998)
6. Rosabeth Moss Kanter *Mary Parker Follett: Prophet of Management* Editor: Pauline Graham (Harvard Business School Press, 1996)
7. Warren Bennis *On Becoming a Leader* (Arrow, 1998)
8. Henri Fayol *General and Industrial Management* English Translation (Pitman, 1967)
9. Henry Mintzberg *The Structure of Organisations* (Prentice Hall, 1979)
10. F.E. Fiedler *Leader Attitudes and Group Effectiveness* (University of Illinois Press, 1958)
11. Warren Bennis *Leaders: Strategies for taking charge* (Harperbusiness, 1997)
12. Jack Welch *What I've learned leading a great company and great people* (Headline, 2001)
13. Charles B. Handy *Understanding Organisations* 4th Edition (Penguin, 1992)
14. Stephen Robbins *Organisational Behaviour* (Prentice Hall, 1993)

Decision-making and information

Decisions, decisions

Decisions dominate our lives. Some are big – which house to buy? Others are small – what to eat for dinner? Some decisions are routine – you have made these hundreds of times before and have probably developed rules or have established answers to make the decisions quickly – should you have sugar or not with your coffee? Others are unfamiliar and happen rarely – should you leave your present job or not?

A manager's day is similarly taken up with decision-making. He or she is continually choosing between alternatives. Resources are limited, so how should they be used most effectively?

The little decisions are usually easy – even if you get them wrong there are no long-term consequences and you can probably change your mind anyway. The large, complex decisions are the ones that can cause real problems:

- they may involve significant resources and you will naturally be worried about getting them wrong
- they may involve many different groups, all with their own view of what they want, so you are probably going to have to reach a compromise
- if you have not made a decision like this before, you may naturally be concerned whether you have the necessary expertise and information to get it right
- some aspects of the decision may be difficult to quantify (How will the players you have picked for the team work together? What will be the impact on morale?).

The scientific approach

There are two approaches to complex and critical decisions. One is to take a scientific approach. This involves clearly defining the objectives, gathering data and analysing it carefully before reaching a conclusion. Imagine a doctor examining you, carefully gathering information about your symptoms before making a diagnosis.

Teletubbies

The scientific approach may not seem particularly well suited to the creative world of the media, but even here, fathering information can be seen as an essential part of the decision making process. The children's programme *Teletubbies* did not just happen to be successful. Its success is based on the findings of thorough market research. As well as observing children at play before developing each show, the market researchers use around 75 families in the UK with cameras on their TVs while their children watch the programmes. This gives the programmers a second-by-second response to the programme content and allows them to assess the children's reactions. *Teletubbies* is now the biggest ever children's export, earning millions in worldwide viewing figures and merchandise. This success is derived from its extensive collection and analysis of data.

amazon.com

Another good example of a logical and rational approach to decision making is the way in which amazon.com, the internet bookstore, was established. The company was set up by Jeff Bezos in1994. Before choosing to start up as an internet bookseller, he analysed around 20 different possible products which he thought could be sold effectively on the internet. Books were particularly appealing because there are so many titles (over 3 million titles are in print at present) and because no traditional bookstore could hope to carry all of these in its shops. The growth of mail-order book selling also showed that people were prepared to buy this product in this way.

Bezos chose Seattle as his location because it has a large pool of people with the necessary technical ability (Microsoft is also based there). It is also near the largest book warehouse in the world. The next stage was to find the right premises and, like many other high tech firms who have gone on to be very successful, such as Apple, he initially set up in the garage of a house!

He then spent a great deal of time and effort building up relationships with suppliers and distributors. These links are the key to his success: they enable the customer to choose from an incredibly large number of titles, and have the books delivered efficiently to the door. Before trading, amazon.com also needed to develop unique order processing software. This was tested by friends and family in a trial six-week period before going live.

Since then the business has grown at an incredible rate (much faster than its business plan), probably because it had such a unique proposition. The company's success was due in no small part to research at each stage and some logical decision making about what would work best.

The intuitive approach

The opposite approach to being rational and scientific is to base decisions purely on intuition – look at a problem, get a feel for it and then decide regardless of what the numbers say. This may be quicker but riskier than a scientific approach.

In reality, a combination of these techniques is likely to be used. Managers may gather data and try to make sense of it, but their gut feelings probably play a role as well. Just think about how most people choose a university and degree course. They plough through the literature and visit the websites, but at the back of their minds they are thinking about whether the name sounds right or whether it feels right. Or look at how we select staff – we look at their applications and compare this with the requirements of the job, but are heavily influenced by the rather unscientific process of the interview.

Decision trees

One tool which is sometimes used in scientific decision making is a decision tree. Constructing a decision tree involves identifying the possible courses of action and their possible outcomes. The likelihood of each outcome is estimated, as is the financial consequence of each one. The manager can then calculate mathematically the most profitable course of action on average.

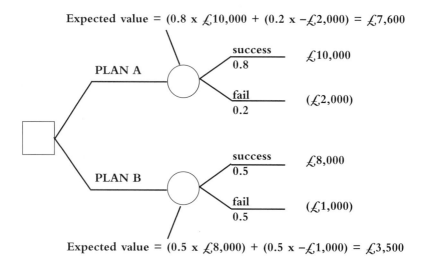

Expected value = (0.8 x £10,000 + (0.2 x −£2,000) = £7,600

PLAN A

success
0.8 ——— £10,000

fail
0.2 ——— (£2,000)

PLAN B

success
0.5 ——— £8,000

fail
0.5 ——— (£1,000)

Expected value = (0.5 x £8,000) + (0.5 x −£1,000) = £3,500

The decision tree above shows two choices facing the business: plan A and plan B. Plan A has an 80% chance of gaining £10,000 and a 20% chance of losing £2,000. On average, this means this plan would lead to a gain of £7,600. For plan B, the average is £3,500. On this basis, plan A would be chosen.

However, the value of the technique relies on the estimates of the probability and on the financial outcomes being accurate. This in turn depends on who estimated them and how they produced these estimates. In an unfamiliar situation, an inexperienced manager's estimates may be very unreliable, for example. In order to push a project through, a manager may overestimate the financial benefits. A further problem with this technique is that it only considers quantifiable data. Factors such as employee morale, the ethics of a situation or the impact on the environment cannot easily be measured in financial terms. Decision trees also fail to take account of managers' attitude to risk. Look at the options below:

- option A: 60% probability of gaining £10m; 40% probability of losing £2 m
- option B: 50% probability of winning £2m; 50% probability of winning £1 m.

According to decision tree analysis, the manager should choose option A because on average this would bring higher returns. However, in reality you may choose option B because this way you cannot lose money; option A has the possibility of very high returns but there is also the chance you might actually lose money. A risk-averse manager might therefore play safe and choose B.

Summary points

- managers face decisions all the time; complex and unfamiliar, or routine

- making decisions involves choosing between alternatives and involves risk

- some managers are more scientific in their approach than others; some rely more on their intuition

- decision trees attempt to quantify the elements of a decision and make it more scientific

THINK about it!

Think about three major decisions you have made in recent years. Now think about how you made these decisions – did you tend to be scientific and logical or more intuitive? What made you choose one option rather than another? Looking back, did you make the right decision in each case? How could it have been made more effectively?

Information management

Information is a resource – the way it is gathered, interpreted and distributed needs to be thought about strategically, not just left for people to make up their own policies in some random manner. If you can collect better data, make better sense of it and ensure the right information gets to the right people at the right time, you are increasing your chances of success.

Information matters, and makes a difference. Bill Gates comments in his book, *Business @ the speed of thought*[1]: 'How you gather, manage and use information will determine whether you win or lose. There are more competitors. There is more information available about them and about the market which is now global. The winners will be the ones who develop a world-class digital nervous system so that information can easily flow through their companies for maximum and constant learning ... no matter what else you have going for you today – smart employees, excellent products, customer goodwill, cash in the bank – you need a fast flow of good information to streamline processes, raise quality, and improve business execution.' Gates believes information management can provide companies with strategic intelligence – what they need to know about their business environment to anticipate change and to design appropriate strategies to succeed.

Managing information properly is not just about investing in IT and making PCs available – it is a question of culture. Managers must be clear on what they want to know. They must be willing to consider how information is kept and must be willing to share ideas and data. In many organisations the fact you have access to some information that others do not have has been seen as a source of personal strength. Managers have been unwilling to share this data because they fear it will undermine their status.

The importance of information to organisations was highlighted when Procter and Gamble (which makes everything from Dove soap to Pringles snacks) admitted it had been spying on its rival Unilever to find out its shampoo secrets in 2001. Three people were dismissed when it was discovered that 'spies' allegedly rifled through Unilever's rubbish to obtain information on new heathcare trends. Unilever demanded compensation, running into tens of millions of dollars. A P&G spokesman claimed the operation 'violated our competitive business information gathering policy', but denied its employees had actually acted illegally. The story was particularly embarrassing because P&G chairman John Pepper has always stressed his interest in 'competitive intelligence' and had even established a secretive arm of the company with its own secret bank accounts and web of information sources. Not long before the P&G revelations, Kraft Food had sued grocery pizza rival Schwan over allegations it had improperly obtained confidential documents on new product launches and strategy. Knowing what your competitors are doing is clearly important and can lead to fairly drastic action at times.

Too much data

The key to effective decision-making is to make sure you have the right information at the right time and in an understandable form. However, you need to avoid collecting data for the sake of it. Not only can this be expensive but also some managers become completely overwhelmed. This can lead to 'paralysis by analysis' – managers spend so long wading through reports and surveys that it actually prevents them from making a decision. To help collect and process information, many companies now have information systems including:

- management information systems – these collect and analyse data and are able to produce regular reports for managers, eg monthly sales figures
- decision support systems – these can help decision-making at all levels in the organisation, eg it may enable users to forecast sales
- expert systems – these are used to offer expert advice on problems, eg a doctor might input a patient's symptoms and use the expert system to diagnose the complaint.

Not enough information

Keeping informed about the external environment is important – you need to be aware of changes in social trends, competitors' actions and the economy, for example. You also need to keep in touch with what is happening internally, as the Nick Leeson case shows. Leeson was a financial currency trader for Barings Bank. Having joined the company in 1982, Leeson worked his way up to become the bank's star trader in Singapore by 1993. In that year he made the company more than £10 m – about 10% of the bank's total profits. In his autobiography Leeson says the culture at the bank was simple: 'we were driven to make profits, profits and more profits'.

In 1994, Leeson's luck ran out and he started to make big losses. He continued to trade, making bigger and riskier deals. In February 1995 a spot audit by Barings discovered his losses amounted to more than £800 m, almost more than the assets of the bank. Leeson had hidden the losses in an account called Error Account 88888. The bank crashed soon after and was sold for £1 to the Dutch Banking and insurance group ING.

Leeson pleaded guilty to fraud and was sentenced to six and a half years in prison. Although he was certainly to blame for the collapse at the bank questions were also asked about how he could be trading and losing such large sums without the bank knowing. There was a lack of internal information and checks which allowed such a disaster to happen.

Don't trust the data?

Many business decisions are based on quantifiable data. We measure, we assess and we base our plans on our findings. However, the actual quality of the decision naturally depends on the quality of the data behind it. If the data is bad the decision is likely to be as well. The extent to which decision can be based on faulty data was highlighted all too well in 2001, when a team of scientists, which was working on a study of the BSE disease in sheep by investigating sheep brains, discovered that they had been wrongly given cow brains in the beginning and had been working on these for the last three years!

Managing knowledge

When we talk of managing information, this does not just mean gathering data from outside the firm. It also means harnessing all the knowledge that exists within the business. Given the growth of the knowledge economy, the management of this internal resource is critical for success. What makes Microsoft so strong? Its experience, its insight, its skills, its knowledge. What is vital in fashion, music, films, publishing, surgery, software design and engineering? Knowledge, creativity and experience. So organisations need to make sure the knowledge it has within the firm is full exploited and mined.

Think about what you know and what all the people around you know – if only we could find ways of combining this knowledge and making it easily accessible to others within the organisation. Far too many people within an organisation spend their time re-inventing the wheel; trying to solve problems that have already been solved by others elsewhere within the firm.

Summary points

- information can help improve decision-making
- ...but you can't always trust the data (remember the cows brains)
- you need to get hold of the information in a legal way
- managing knowledge is a key challenge of the 21st century; the ability to know what your customers want and to tap into the experience of employees can provide a firm with a competitive advantage

THINK
about it!

Think about a major decision you have made recently or are in the process of making, eg choosing a university course, buying a car, buying new clothes.

Where did you get information from to make your decision? How long did you take in the process? What made you finally decide? Would you say this was a scientific decision or not?

Reference

1.   Bill Gates *Business @ the speed of thought* (Penguin, 2000)

Marketing

In the beginning, there was marketing

First and foremost, a business needs customers. To have a customer, you have to have something to offer them. This may be a physical product like a car, or it may be a service like financial advice. But whatever it is, it has got to be something they want. So one of the first rules of business is to know what your customers really want to buy; then you have to provide it. This is known as 'market orientation'.

MARKET ORIENTATION

Sounds simple? In theory it is, but consistently providing what customers want is not so easy. Many businesses have very little idea of what their customers really want. They carry on doing what they always have done or what they like to do almost regardless of their customers' preferences. This approach is called 'product orientation'. If customers don't have much choice elsewhere, or if what the firm is offering is good enough for the moment the business may survive and even prosper for a while.

PRODUCT ORIENTATION

Take the famous Model T Ford launched in 1914. This was the first mass produced car, and it sold because Ford could offer it at a price which no one else could match ($250) and because there was almost no competition. Customers put up with the fact that there was no variety and the Model T sold over 15 million cars (even though it was 'available in any colour so long as it's black'!). However, life changed dramatically when Alfred Sloan took over General Motors and started to offer all kinds of optional features. Not only that, General Motors developed a range of products and brands (Buick, Chevrolet and Cadillac) so you could move up the range as your income increased. Variety won through and Ford's sales collapsed.

The starting point for a successful business is therefore to think of things from the customer's perspective. This is the essence of marketing. In the 1970s, the drinks company Diageo realised that there was a growing market in the UK for wine drinking, and that the average wine drinker was not well-informed but wanted to appear knowledgeable. This led to the creation of 'Le Piat d'Or', a wine supposedly loved by the French even though it was not even sold in France! By 2001, the company realised that British wine drinkers had become much better informed about wine and were no longer impressed by the French association. The product was re-branded and repositioned to meet changing tastes and attitudes; an excellent example of a firm which monitors the market and changes its approach accordingly – ie a market-orientated business.

What are you offering your customers?

Customers want value. This means you must offer them benefits at a price they are willing and able to pay. These benefits may include:

- better productivity – your product may do something faster or more effectively than the alternatives. Remember the Duracell bunnies which kept on drumming long after its rivals stopped? Duracell offered longer-lasting batteries
- ease of use – the number of programmes on most washing machines is bewildering; some customers would happily pay for a simpler version. Notice how PC and video manufacturers have now made it much easier for you to set up the machine once you buy it
- convenience – many of us will pay for a firm which makes life easier for us; consider the growth of microwaveable food and home delivery shopping
- less risk – this is where the value of brands come in; you can rely on certain names, and even if it goes wrong, you trust them to fix it
- an experience – eating at The Ivy restaurant or the Hard Rock Cafe provides an experience beyond just eating food.

When we talk of benefits we mean the perceived benefit of our consumers – what matters is whether customers *think* there is any benefit, not whether there *actually* is one. If you think that anti-wrinkle cream helps, then it provides a perceived benefit; it you think the sun cream developed in the 'laboratoire' is worth paying 30% more for than an ordinary cream then it is; if pine fresh cleaner is better in your view (and to your nose) than any another, then it obviously is and the producer has identified a perceived benefit.

Summary points

- marketing begins and ends with the customer
- you need to understand your customers; they don't always behave the way you expect
- you need to offer them what they want (which may not be the same as you want!)
- you may be successful now; this does not mean you will keep your customers if something else comes along. To continue to be successful, you must monitor your markets and customer needs

THINK about it!

Think of a shop you buy from regularly. Would you describe this store as market- or product-orientated? Justify your answer.

What is marketing about?

Ask most people what marketing involves, and they would say 'advertising'. To some extent they would be right, but marketing is far far more than this. Marketing provides the crucial link between the organisation and its customers. It involves finding out what those customers want, what they really want to buy. It involves assessing the competition and the nature of the market to see which segments to compete in. And it involves working with the other functions of the firm such as operations to decide how those needs can be met efficiently. It promotes the product to its customers and ensures it is distributed effectively. And it ensures the organisation's objectives are met at the same time.

A famous American writer, Ralph Waldo Emerson once wrote, 'If a man write a better book, preach a better sermon or make a better mousetrap than his neighbour though he build his house in the woods, the world will make a beaten path to his door.' If only this were true. In fact, this is now known as the 'Mousetrap Fallacy'. Having a good mousetrap is not good enough – people need to know about it, the price has to be right and it has to be in the right place (note the middle of the forest doesn't sound ideal). All of these are marketing activities and are essential to the sale of a product and repeat business.

A two-way process

Marketing should be seen as a two-way, ongoing process: listening to customers, responding to their needs and keeping in touch as their needs change. Marketing should be seen as a mutually beneficial exchange process. Mutually beneficial because both sides should win; it is not just about the firm gaining at the expense of the customer or the customer gaining value and the company losing money. It is about both sides walking away from a transaction thinking they have achieved their goals. You have your profit. The customer feels he/she has had value for money.

One of the best definitions of marketing comes from Hugh Davidson[1]: 'Offensive marketing involves every employee in building superior customer value very efficiently for above average profits.' This elegant definition demonstrates that marketing:

- involves every employee; everything that everyone does can have an impact on the final quality of the product and therefore can influence the customers' perception of the business
- sets out to build. Marketing involves developing products, developing brand image and developing loyalty. It is long-term and constructive, not destructive
- builds 'superior customer value'. It is not about matching competitors. It is about beating them by offering something extraordinary to customers
- aims to be efficient, not wasteful
- seeks above-average profit; marketing, if conducted properly, should enable your business to excel, not to be average.

Watch your back

The dynamic nature of business makes success a fragile creature. Theodore Levitt once wrote about the dangers of 'marketing myopia' (shortsightedness) – firms can easily lose sight of what is going on around them and find themselves hopelessly out of date. They need to be constantly watching their backs. In the 1970s, for example, IBM lost track of developments in the computer market, wrongly believing that personal computers would not take off. The result was that the company put most of its resources into mainframes (big computers for firms) leaving the way open in the home PC market to the competition. IBM read the market incorrectly and paid the price for many years to come.

New products arrive, customers demand more and firms have to find their space in changing markets. Even a market so seemingly traditional as book retailing has undergone radical transformation as market conditions change. Shops such as Borders now sell books, CDs, videos and newspapers as well as offering an in-store cafe. The main competitors in book retailing now see themselves as leisure environments, not just shops. They want us to go 'destination shopping': to browse, to read, to drink and to emerge, inspired and refreshed, and with a lot less money in our pockets a few hours later.

What I did on my holiday

When I first went to Greece on holiday a few years ago, I had an excellent meal; the bill came and it was only a few pounds. I was very satisfied and thanked the waiter. He then brought me a free brandy. I was delighted with this unexpected gift and went back to this restaurant to eat every night of my stay.

The restaurant had offered me good food at a reasonable price and given me a gift for eating with them – this exceeded my expectations and won my loyalty.

The second time I visited Greece (but a different area this time), the same thing happened, but this time I took the free drink for granted. I was not so impressed. The third time I went back to Greece there was no free drink with the meal and I felt cheated. What had originally been a fantastic 'extra' had become 'the norm' – I wanted more! The world moves on, and to succeed firms must keep pace with it. To satisfy and to exceed our expectations, firms have to keep improving to match and improve on what others are doing. The stakes just keep getting higher.

Summary points

- marketing is not just advertising – it is much broader than this

- success can only come through an understanding of the customer

- everyone in the business is involved in marketing to some extent

- markets change and firms must monitor these changes to prevent falling behind

- customers want value for money

- customers' expectations keep increasing. The more you give them, the more they expect next time!

THINK about it!

Markets change all the time. Products rise and fall in popularity. Identify two products or markets which are booming at present and two which are in decline. Try to think why this is the case for each of the products. What is your prediction for the next big growth product?

Market research

At the heart of a successful business is the ability to produce a good or service which customers want and which represents good or, hopefully, excellent value for money. To do this often requires effective market research. The aim of such research is to identify existing customer needs, and if possible highlight future trends. The research may be primary (finding out data for the first time, eg through questionnaires) or secondary (using existing sources such as newspaper surveys). Compare a Saga holiday for older customers with an 18–30 holiday for younger people, and you'll soon see the need to change the marketing according to your target audience!

What market opportunities exist?

What strategies should the firm adopt to exploit the opportunities?

How successful have these strategies been; what actions now need to be taken?

Uses of market research

Successful organisations or individuals see market research as a vital part of their activities. They use every opportunity they can to embrace their customers and find out how they use their products, what they think of them and so on. Procter and Gamble, the huge American consumer goods producer, claims that consumer understanding is 'the heart and start' of everything it does. It set up one of the world's first market research departments in 1924 and now receives comments from more than 4.5 million consumers annually. It has set up a 'consumer corner' on the web where selected users post messages about their experiences with P&G products. The company also uses camera crews in people's homes to collect footage of real life.

Other obsessives like Sam Walton, the founder of Wal-Mart, used to read every letter of complaint himself to find out what it was that *his* customers (yes, he took it personally) did not like. Some leaders like to go out and visit their stores and talk to their customers to experience things first hand. At Kwik Fit, the company's attention to customer satisfaction is highlighted by the amount of post-service research it does. Its Customer Service Unit based in West Central Scotland calls more than 5,000 customers per day within 72 hours of their visit to a Kwik Fit centre. This ensures the company is completely up to date with their customers' views and that any problems can be identified quickly. Perhaps not surprisingly, given this attention to finding out what customers think, the company's customer satisfaction rating is over 98.2%; many other companies are more than happy with 60%.

The Kwik Fit Philosophy states: 'At Kwik Fit, the most important person is the customer and it must be the aim of us all to give 100% customer satisfaction 100% of the time. Our continued success depends on the loyalty of our customers. We are committed to offering them the best value for money with a fast, courteous and professional service. We offer the highest quality products and guarantees. We at Kwik-Fit recognise that our people in our Centres are the all important contact with the customers and they are the key to the success of the Kwik Fit group'. (Tom Farmer, founder of Kwik Fit)

At my local branch of Pret A Manger I recently saw the following card that impressed me:

> My name is Phil. I'm the general manager at Bicester.
> My Team and I meet every morning. We will discuss the points you've raised ... the good, the bad and the ugly. If we can deal with it ourselves, we will. If we can't I will forward your card to Andrew R. at the office. I know he will do what he can.
> Either way. Thanks.
> PRET A MANGER, Bicester

You can't say fairer than that – the company wants to know what we think and creates the impression they will do something about it.

What is infuriating is when companies appear to be interested but do nothing with the information they have gathered. I get very depressed when visiting hotels that have asked for your views in a comment book, only to see that exactly the same problems still exist one or two years later. If they are not going to do anything about it, why bothering asking? It only disappoints.

Information Technology

The gathering of information is, of course, undergoing a revolution. With the growth of information technology, the storage and analysis of data can now occur on a scale that could never have been imagined a few years ago. Storecards have been a particularly important development because they have allowed stores to link what you buy with details of who you are. Previously they could track what was being bought via electronic point of sales systems. Now they can trace exactly what sort of person or household is buying what combination of goods. This can influence everything from the way a product is promoted to where it is displayed in the store.

The relatively low cost and increasing power of information technology (IT) enables firms to undertake 'data mining' much more effectively than in the past. They can trawl the data for trends and links between who buys what and when. One major supermarket chain was recently considering dropping a particular type of cheese, only to discover that its major buyers were also buyers of other very high profit margin items; the cheese was kept to keep this type of buyer happy.

Not all managers use research – some simply base their decisions on gut feeling – they think they know what customers want, and in some cases they think they know better than customers themselves. The managing director of First Leisure once said that people do not know what they want to do to enjoy themselves until they are shown the possibilities – did we really know we wanted to go to an Irish theme pub, go bowling or go ice skating until someone built one of these facilities nearby? Managers may even be bold enough to ignore their research findings. Akio Morita at Sony, for example, was said to have ignored much of the research that suggested that the Walkman would be unsuccessful – he knew it could work and pushed the project on.

In general, undertaking research can reduce the risk of making decisions. Obviously the better the research, the more likely it is you will get it right, so you need to think about issues such as the sample size and way in which questions are phrased. Research can be wrong, as Sony found out; this is not necessarily because the concept of research is wrong, but because of the way it has been carried out. For example, BSN, a French food company, encountered problems with its market research in the 1990s when it was considering launching Danone yoghurt in Japan. Extensive testing occurred which confirmed the product should do well, but when the launch actually happened sales were much lower than expected. Why? Because the researchers had not taken into account the politeness of the average Japanese customer – when asked whether they liked the yoghurt the Japanese consumer (who was much more used to the liquid drinking yoghurts than the solid yoghurts of Danone) said 'yes' even when a) they actively hated it and b) couldn't understand how to eat it!

Summary points

▶ market research can help reduce the risk in making marketing decisions

▶ market research may be primary or secondary – ie using new or existing data

▶ market research does not guarantee success; it can help make more informed decisions, but mistakes can still be made

You are the commissioning editor of a major publishing company. You are considering a proposal from a writer for a new book. The author is well known but this is the first thriller he has written. Two reviewers whom you trust like it and you like it as well (and you read a lot of thrillers!). Your boss has suggested you should do more research before going ahead. Do you do more research or not? What does your decision depend on?

Market research in action: Daewoo

In the 1990s Daewoo, a major Korean industrial conglomerate producing everything from ships to electrical goods, decided to enter the UK car market. This involved a major investment and risk, given that consumers had no previous experience of Daewoo cars and the company had no retail or servicing network. However, Daewoo was determined to turn these apparent weaknesses into virtues by developing a totally new approach to the selling of cars. They succeeded in gaining a foothold in the market in an impressively short space of time. The company did this by undertaking detailed market research.

Following an initial study of the market, Daewoo categorised sales of cars in the UK as follows :

- the core establishment – cars which do not have to be justified to the neighbours, eg Ford
- the European establishment – cars which have been in the market for several years but the public are still slightly reluctant to buy, eg Citroen
- the Japanese – cars which are gradually becoming accepted after over 20 years, eg Toyota
- the emergents – the non-Japanese Asian makes such as Proton, which have enormous potential but have not gained a secure foothold in the market
- the bargain basement which offer a low price proposition, eg Robin Reliant.

Daewoo decided to base its approach on customer satisfaction, and declared that its aim was to become the most customer-focused car company in the world. 'Volvo stands for safety, Volkswagen stands for reliability and Daewoo is going to stand for customer focus,' said Daewoo's Marketing Director. The first stage of Daewoo's campaign was to raise awareness. Very few people had ever heard of the company and so before it could start to reassure its customers, it had to make itself known in the market.

With a starting point of just 4% awareness, the company addressed the Dae – who? problem with a communication strategy that concentrated on two messages: Daewoo's status as one of the world's largest corporations and its huge range of high quality and high-tech products. Its humorous campaign, 'Daewoo, the biggest car company you've never heard of' emphasised the friendly and approachable nature of the firm, while also highlighting the fact that Daewoo ranked among the world's largest 30 industrial companies.

The next stage was to discover more about customer attitudes towards car buying and develop the Daewoo proposition as the most customer-focused car company. The company created a response campaign, asking people for their likes and dislikes in car buying. These initial responses gave them valuable market research data as well as a database of real prospects (potential purchasers). At one point 45,000 people tried to call the Daewoo hotline in one hour – a response second only to Children in Need.

A guinea pig programme was also developed alongside the response campaign with 200 respondents given cars to test-drive for 12 months following the launch. These people reported once a month with their findings on the car and servicing arrangements, providing Daewoo with first-hand and continuous feedback.

All initial respondents were sent a questionnaire asking for more detailed questions and, because the sample of the buying population was so large, the findings had real credibility. The findings of the research highlighted that:
- car salespeople were unpopular
- high pressure selling is strongly disliked
- women play an increasing role in the buying decision
- customers want courtesy, free servicing, free road tax and family entertainment in the showroom.

As a result of these findings Daewoo developed the Daewoo Manifesto: Direct, Hassle free, Peace of Mind and Courtesy.

The launch in 1995 was also accompanied by the announcement that Daewoo would exchange the first 1000 retail customers' cars for new cars after one year. This offer would quickly create a used car market and was an incentive for customers who were uncertain about a Daewoo to make a purchase.

Unlike most of their competitors, Daewoos have a fixed inclusive price; there are no hidden extras. The Daewoo price includes:
- delivery to home or office
- number plates
- 12 month's road fund licence
- full tank of fuel

- 3 year/60,000 mile comprehensive warranty
- 3 years' free servicing
- 3 years' comprehensive AA cover
- 30 days peace of mind (exchange or refund)
- security registration
- mobile telephone for personal security
- delivery and collection of car for servicing
- courtesy car during servicing

Another major difference in the Daewoo approach is that the staff in Daewoo retail outlets are 'customer advisers' not salespeople, and are salaried rather than commissioned so customers are not pressurised into a sale. Prices are fixed so there is no haggling and the advisers do not hassle customers; it is up to the customer to start any discussion. All the information about the company and its cars is available, including an outline of finance and insurance packages, from user friendly touch-screen modules in the outlets.

Summary points

- Daewoo thoroughly researched the UK car market before entering

- the company's strategy was built on its market research findings

- it found a unique position within the market because it understood the market so well

 **THINK about it!**

You have £15,000 to spend on a new car. Decide which type of car you would buy with this money. Justify your answer. What are the main three factors that influence your decision to buy a particular type of new car? What are the three main sources of information you would use to help you decide which car to buy?

Segmenting the market

The simplest way to serve a market is to provide the same thing for everyone. This makes it easy in terms of production – you churn out the same thing day after day. The only problem with this approach is that customers don't always want the same thing as everyone else! This means it's usually worth looking for segments in the market – groups of similar needs and wants – and then deciding which segment or segments to target. You can then adjust your marketing according to the needs of the segments you are serving.

So, how do you segment the market? You look for characteristics which groups of consumers have in common and which allow you to modify what you offer to serve them better. Segmentation may be based on a wide range of criteria, such as:

- gender: witness the growth of men's magazines such as *FHM* in recent years and the increase in male 'grooming' products
- size: Evans shops serve the larger woman; High and Mighty is a store for tall and large men
- region: newspapers often produce regional editions focusing on, for example, local football matches.

You may also segment by the type of customer you are serving. The DIY market, for example, can be split into the trade and household sector. The trade market in the UK is worth about £9bn and is dominated by Wolseley, Travis Perkins and Saint Gobain who have about 50% of the market combined. The home market is worth about £12bn and is dominated by Focus, B&Q and Homebase.

Alternatively, you may try and segment by considering why people buy the product, ie, what is their motivation? In the case of chocolate, for example, some people buy it as a comfort food, some buy it to share with others, others buy it to reward themselves, some buy it as a present. All of these segments create market opportunities – the chance to change what you do to develop a service which delights them.

Sometimes you don't know your consumer

When undertaking an analysis of the market it may be important to distinguish between the customer (who buys) and the consumer (who uses). The child may want the toy, the parent may buy it; hence pester power campaigns designed specifically to get the child to irritate the parents so much he or she will give in. In the case of industrial products (goods or services sold to other firms to be used in their process), the buyers may be professional purchasers; they themselves may never use the machines. Textbooks are often ordered by teachers, paid for by schools and, hopefully, read by students. Marketing must therefore take into account the needs of the buyers as well as the users. Sometimes the difference between the two can cause difficulties, as Pilkington plc discovered.

At the start of the 21st century, Pilkington plc invented a revolutionary self-cleaning glass. Called Pilkington Activ, this glass has a coating that absorbs the ultra violet light from the sun, causing a reaction that breaks down dirt. The coating causes rainwater to wash over the glass like a sheet, rather than forming droplets, and seeps away the dirt. The potential is huge – vast glass office blocks not needing windows to be cleaned! The problem is that the people who will benefit are not the ones responsible for buying the glass in the first place. The builders who install the glass tend to look for the best deal they can and Activ is not cheap! Builders are only likely to install this if they have to, and a law insisting on self-cleaning glass is unlikely!

Summary points

- ▶ segmentation can enable you to provide a tailor-made product
- ▶ different segments will want different things; if you understand the segments fully, you can provide a better service
- ▶ the consumer and customer may be different people and may not agree on what they want

THINK about it!

The market for clothes is clearly segmented in terms of sizes; eg for women, 8,10,12 etc, for men there are waist sizes 30, 32, 34 etc. Why are there not more sizes available, eg 9 and 11 for women or 30.5, 31.5 for men?

Market analysis

Effective marketing is based on a good understanding of the market. If you know what is happening in your sector, you are more likely to make the right decisions. You need to understand the nature of the market very precisely to decide how and where you are going to compete. Take the chocolate market – this can be broken up into various segments, such as:

- the impulse buy – in the shop you see a bar of chocolate and buy
- the present – boxed chocolates you buy to give to someone else
- the sharing – chocolates you buy and hand around to others
- the eat later – bars of chocolate you are buying to eat later.

Competing in each of these segments will bring different challenges and requirements. This is why an effective analysis of the market is important, otherwise you are likely to have the wrong tools for the job.

Boston Matrix

Tools of market analysis include product portfolio analysis and the product life cycle. Product portfolio analysis examines all of a firm's existing products. There are various models that set out to do this. One of the most famous is the Boston Matrix, which assesses products on the basis of their market share and the growth of the market as a whole. Products are plotted in the matrix given their position on these rankings. Four categories of products can then be identified:

- Cash cows – these products have a high market share in low-growth markets, for example, a dominant product in a mature market such as Heinz Tomato Ketchup. For this type of product there is limited room for further growth within the market but it is likely to be profitable; much of the marketing work has been done and sales are still high. These funds from cash cows may be put into new products or the firm may try to diversify.
- Question marks – these are also called 'oil rigs' or 'problem children'. These are products with a small market share in a fast-growing market. The overall market is attractive because it is growing so fast, but this product has yet to establish itself. It may need investment to promote it but, over time, if nurtured and cared for, it may become a success. This might be a new model of digital camera, for example.
- Stars – this type of product has a high market share in a high-growth market. It has all kinds of potential but may need protection from 'me-too' products. This could be the latest successful quiz show programme.
- Dogs – these products have low market share in low-growth markets. A firm must decide if it is worth continuing with a dog product. If it is it will probably need heavy investment to turn it around. Products such as Ovaltine, Lucozade and Tango have successfully been repositioned and revived. Not all dogs are dead dogs.

The Boston Matrix

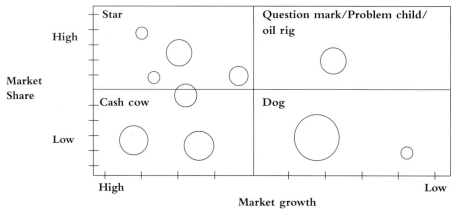

(Each circle represents a product; the area of the circle represents the turnover of each product)

Product life cycle

Another common model used in marketing analysis is the product life cycle. This measures the sales of a product over time. The different stages in a product's life are categorised as:

- **pre-launch**, when the product is being developed. Protoypes may be being developed and tested. When Dyson was working on his revolutionary vacuum cleaner, he made at least 5000 prototypes before he got it right
- **introduction**, when the product is launched on to the market. Sales are low at this stage, but the level of promotion usually needs to be high. This means there is often an overall cash outflow
- **growth**; this occurs when sales are increasing fairly rapidly. Sales of DVDs are in the growth phase at present
- **maturity**; this occurs when sales growth is slow. Sales of CDs are now maturing in the UK, as are those of mobile phones
- **decline**; this occurs when sales fall. The quiz show 'Who wants to be a Millionaire?' was developed and first shown in the UK. It was launched in the US in the summer of 1999; by early 2000 it dominated US TV ratings with as many as 28 million viewers and was aired four times a week. By 2000 this was reduced to two nights a week. In the UK, viewing figures per show were down to nine million in 2001, way down from its peak of 19 million in March 1999.

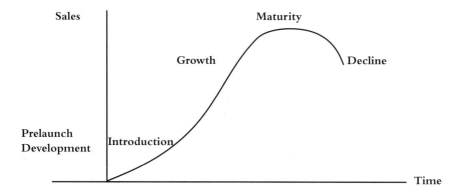

Summary points

▶ market analysis involves an examination of a market

▶ by analysing a market, the right strategy can be chosen

▶ market analysis involves product portfolio analysis and the product life cycle

▶ the Boston Matrix assesses a firm's products in terms of their market share and their market growth

▶ the product life cycle model highlights the need for different marketing activities at different stages

THINK about it!

Go to your bathroom and look at the different products in there – toothpaste, soaps, shampoos, conditioners.

■ Write down who makes each of the products – do you notice anything here?

■ Write down where you think the brand is in terms of the Boston Matrix (eg cash cow, dog, question mark, star). Why have you put it here? What would you do with the product if you were the brand manager?

The Marketing Mix

The price, the price, the price

Ask many people what determines whether something sells or not, and they will often reply: 'the price'. 'Cut the price to boost sales and increase your profits' seems glaringly obvious. But if you observe how customers actually behave, you will see that price is often not the major consideration. And there are times when we deliberately go for the more expensive rather than the cheaper option.

I was recently talking to a football fan who had paid nearly £20 for a ticket to a Tottenham Hotspur match. Value for money? He thought so − it was a big game with two of his favourites sides and, as he said, he would have been prepared to pay much more than that to get tickets. He didn't shop around for cheaper tickets to another match − he wanted to see Tottenham Hotspur.

When you are going for a meal, do you always choose the place with the cheapest food? I suspect not. The price, therefore, does not always have a big impact on our decision to buy. Of course there are times when price is more important − eg, if you are working on a tight budget or if there are goods where the price can easily be compared − but we are often not as price-sensitive as we may like to think.

If it isn't just the price, what is it?

There are literally hundreds of things which influence why we buy something. The different elements that influence your purchase have been labelled the Marketing Mix, and are often categorised under four headings:

- **Price** − what you pay, any discounts you might get, the credit period you are offered
- **Product** − this includes the product's specifications, what it does, its reliability, its serviceability
- **Promotion** − this involves all the different ways in which a firm communicates with its potential market, eg advertising, sales promotions (such as discounts and special offers), the salesforce and public relations. But beware, if you are going to use promotions, plan them properly − unlike Hoover. In the late 1990s, Hoover offered two free return flights to Europe or America to any customers who bought any of its vacuum cleaners, washing machines or other household appliances worth more than £100. The company miscalculated: most consumers bought vacuum cleaners costing about £120 at a time when the cheapest pair of tickets to New York cost £500! The firm was inundated with around 20,000

applications for free flights within the first ten months of campaign, and many customers had to wait for their tickets. The disastrous campaign cost the company over £48 million!

- **Place** – this is how the product is distributed from the manufacturer to the purchaser, eg is it sold direct or is it sold via wholesalers and retailers?

What is a product anyway?

A product may be a tangible good, such as a car, or an intangible service, such as education. A product has three dimensions:

- the core product – this describes the essential benefit it provides, eg a washing machine cleans clothes. When thinking of marketing a product, you must consider the alternatives to the core benefit. Unilever recently launched myhome.com because it appreciated that what people actually want is clean clothes. The only reason they buy a washing machine is because it helps them achieve that aim. If you can get the clothes cleaned any other way this is a substitute offering. Myhome.com is an internet-based service by which you can order someone in to clean your house and clothes
- the tangible product – this involves the particular features a product offers, eg for a washing machine it may involve size, spin speed, energy usage and design. Firms which excel in product design include Black and Decker in cordless applications (drills, screwdrivers etc); Bose in audio equipment and Braun in shavers
- the augmented product – this involves all the additional benefits a product may provide, such as home delivery, a 5-year guarantee or free advice.

A firm may compete on any of these levels. You may want a PC because it will help you produce your reports more effectively. The reason you choose a particular model may be because of its processing speed, its screen size or its price. On an augmented level you may buy a brand because of its image, because you get free advice, free guarantee service or home delivery.

How do we get the right marketing mix?

The marketing mix should be relatively obvious if the planning beforehand has been done properly. I recently sent a proposal for a book to the publishers which was rejected because the readers could not work on how it was going to be positioned in the market – was it for use by the lecturers? By the students as background reading? As a main textbook? It was simply not clear what it as trying to do. I went back to the drawing board, clarified my target audience and suddenly it was a lot clearer what should and should not be in it, how long it should be, how it should be written and how it could be promoted.

So forget about the mix until you have checked out the following stages:

- do you have a clear marketing objective – do you know what you are hoping to achieve in terms of sales and profits?
- have you analysed the market effectively – are you clear what segments exist in the market, which ones you are targetting and how you will position yourself relative to the existing competitors?
- are you clear on your strategy? Are you fighting in a niche or mass market, at the top end of the market, or as a mid-market product?

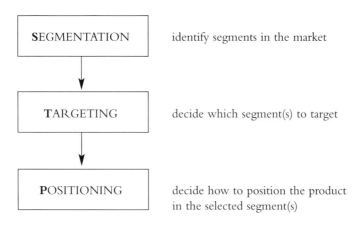

SEGMENTATION	identify segments in the market
TARGETING	decide which segment(s) to target
POSITIONING	decide how to position the product in the selected segment(s)

Easyjet vs British Airways?

Easyjet and British Airways are obviously competing in the air transport market, but pursue very different strategies. Easyjet have pursued the low-cost approach. This therefore has implications for the marketing mix. Whatever it does, it needs to keep costs down to fit with its low-cost positioning; this explains why it decided to use local airports rather than the more expensive ones such as Heathrow and Gatwick. It also explains its no-frills approach, such as a very limited service on board and its push for online booking to cut costs further. Up until 2002, it operated a fleet of just 26 planes flying 35 routes. BA, by comparison, decided to target business executives. In this segment price is less crucial – what matters is the quality of service. BA actually took seats out of its planes so each passenger had more leg room (for which they are charged more); while EasyJet looks for limited creature comforts BA wanted to maximise the pleasure and facilities factor for its customers. Interestingly, following poor results BA has recently announced a change in its strategy to attack the low-cost airlines more directly.

Corporate objectives	eg to boost profits by 20% over two years
Marketing objectives	eg to boost sales by 40% over two years
Marketing strategy	eg to focus on the top end niche of the UK market
Marketing Mix	eg limited exclusive distribution, high price

The marketing planning process

Fit with the strategy

The marketing mix must clearly fit with the strategy selected. The different elements must also fit with each other. A heavily branded product is usually expensive and sold in controlled outlets. A mass market, standardised product is usually distributed more widely and has a lower price. Haagen Dazs, for example, is clearly positioned as a super-premium ice cream. Its ingredients include chocolate from Benelux, vanilla from Madagascar, coffee from Brazil, strawberries from Oregon and nuts from Hawaii and Switzerland. The text on the packaging states that it is the world's best ice cream. It has used award-winning press adverts, artistically shot – often in black and white and featuring attractive semi-nude couples entwined in exotic poses while feeding each other Haagen Dazs ice cream. The advertising promotes an adult, up-market, glamorous positioning for this super-premium ice cream which justifies a high price. The elements combine successfully and reinforce each other. If these elements do not combine successfully the marketing package does not work.

Summary points

▶ the marketing mix is the combination of factors which influence your decision to buy a good or services

▶ the price may count but it is not the only thing that matters; the role of the price must be analysed in the context of the rest of the mix

▶ the marketing mix should be derived from the overall marketing strategy

---

THINK about it!

Without checking, write down the prices of the following items. Find out what they really are and compare the differences. What does this tell you about the importance of price in shopping? Does your awareness differ from item to item? Why?

- Your brand of toothpaste
- A pint of milk from your local shop
- The quarterly gas bill
- Your last mobile phone bill
- A colour television licence
- A litre of petrol
- A Dyson vacuum cleaner

The brand

The role of the brand in modern society is crucial. Firms spend millions of pounds in building up the brand image, thereby creating an asset for an organisation which can form the basis of a competitive advantage; eg, BMW bought the Rolls Royce name (the name alone) for £40 m. A brand stands for a whole series of values that customers can identify with. When customers buy a Harley Davidson, they are buying so much more than a motorbike; they are buying a lifestyle. A Harley rider is rebellious, believes in the open road and is wild at heart. A Yamaha may be efficient but it has no heart. A Harley growls; a Yamaha hums.

A brand attracts customers and locks them in. You want to be seen wearing Gucci because you identify with its values and want to be associated with the Gucci name. You wear the Manchester United shirt because on a rainy Sunday afternoon playing for your village team you are David Beckham. Brands command loyalty and enable firms to justify a higher price.

The brand can also act as an ambassador when a company offers new products or enters new markets. Just look at the way Virgin has used its name and values to enter a whole stream of markets, from records to Cola, pensions to railways, airlines to wedding outfits. Stelios Haji-Ioannou, the founder of EasyJet airlines, has set up up Easycar (car rental), EasyInternet Café, EasyMoney (financial services) and Easydotcom. The concept of Sweden's Absolut Vodka in its now famous clear bottle was developed long before it ever produced any vodka. The company focused on the brand and then developed the product. Goren Lundqvist, the company's president, says that Absolut's wit rather than its taste is the reason for the product's success.

The strength of brand values can be seen in a number of recent advertising campaigns ('if Smirnoff made ...', 'if Carlsberg ran a bank ...'), that show what might happen if the values of the brand were transferred to new sectors.

From a customer's point of view, a brand makes life easier. You don't have to worry about shopping around and making all those difficult choices between items. As Unilever's chairman Niall Fitzgerald says: 'A brand is a storehouse of trust. That matters more and more as choices multiply. People want to simplify their lives'.

Brand building

The development of the brand may come through promotions, but it can also be through the way the parent company acts. According to Howard Schultz, the chairman of Starbucks coffee shop chain: 'The brand has to start with the culture and naturally extend to our customers ... It begins with investing in employees, not advertising'. In 20 years, Starbucks has grown from 18 retail shops to over 4400; in that time it has only spent around $20 m on traditional advertising. Nevertheless, by building a distinctive culture, Starbucks has come to represent the 'third place' between work and home. 'We have benefited by the fact that our stores are reliable, safe and consistent, where people can take a break.'

Nike and the swoosh

One of the greatest examples of brand building in recent years is Nike. Nike has managed to build the 'swoosh' (which represents the wing of Nike, the Greek goddess of victory) into one of the best-known brands in the world. Its appeal stretches from the streets to the stars – it knows no boundaries. The company's strategy of building superior products around popular athletes and its brilliant 'Just Do It' advertising campaign have changed the face of sports marketing. It has associated itself with some of the most famous names in sport such as Tiger Woods, Michael Jordan and André Agassi, so that those who wear Nike are associating themselves with these heroes as well.

As it says on its website, 'Nike has always known the truth – it's not so much the shoes but where they take you'. The company does not just sell sportswear – it markets a way of life, a sports culture, a Just Do It attitude. It is built on a real passion for sport and a disregard for convention. It believes in hard work and serious sports performance. Interestingly, one of the biggest problems facing the firm is its own success – it is so well-known that it has moved from being a maverick to a mainstream player. As its founder says: 'Now that we've grown so large there's a fine line between being a rebel and being a bully'. To overcome this, Nike has created various sub-brands to keep it youthful and distinctive.

When the brand lets you down: Bic

While a brand can send out all the right signals to consumers, it can also act as a liability if the image is wrong. In the late 1980s four new colognes for men and women were introduced. Nothing too unusual in this – new brands are being launched all the time in this market – except the brand name in this case was Bic. Bic spent over £13 m for its marketing campaign, but disappointing sales contributed to a 22% drop in profits. Its advertising focused mainly on the shape of the package (similar to a cigarette lighter), not the fragrance. The problem was that all of the associations with Bic pens (plastic, cheap and disposable) did not fit with the target market's aspirations.

Reviving the brand

An interesting brand decision in the 1990s was the deliberate choice by VW to keep the Skoda brand name. Although Skoda had once had a very strong brand name, particularly in the Czech Republic where it originated, it had become associated in the West with poor quality and a down-market image. It would have been easier at first glance to drop the Skoda image, but VW persevered and as the company rebuilt its reputation for good quality, reliable cars, and the fact that this contradicted everyone's expectations was built into its advertising.

As this shows, a brand is not a static thing. Brands can mature and develop. Another successful repositioning in recent years was Pringle, which became the new trendy knitwear maker. Out went the tired old image, as Pringle became the first choice for celebrities such as Robbie Williams, David Beckham and Madonna. The brand, once known for its golf sweaters, was bought by a Hong Kong textile group and was losing about £3 m a year. Its Scottish factory was facing closure until new designers were brought in to produce a new look and its marketing was adjusted.

Branding the internet

The value of the brand has become particularly important in the world of the internet. The internet provides access to literally thousands of products. Consumers can find substitute products at the click of a button. But how to choose? How do you know whether the business is reliable? The brand is the key. It is interesting how some internet brands such as yahoo! and amazon.com have established themselves in a relatively short period of time. Their job has been to convince users of their reliability to build up loyalty.

The negative aspect of the brand

For a forceful attack on brands, read *No Logo* by Naomi Klein[2]. She argues that brands represent a major proportion of a company's value and its largest source of profits, and that they are used to exploit the consumer. Companies are switching from making products to marketing dreams, lifestyles and images. Such companies offer 'a Barbie world for adults' says Klein. They create the world around us: 'Powerful brands no longer just advertise in a magazine, they control its content'; they pervade every aspect of life from clothes to schools to healthcare. Her argument is that brands have come to represent 'a fascist state where all salute the logo and have little opportunity for criticism because our newspapers, television stations, internet servers, streets and retail spaces are all controlled by multinational corporate interests'.

Also, brands must not think of themselves as safe and everlasting. In 1991, Ratners ran a chain of very successful jewellery shops. Then Gerald Ratner made a humorous after-dinner speech in which he said that his products were 'total crap' and claimed that a Marks and Spencers sandwich lasted longer than some of his company's jewellery. What was meant as a joke at a dinner was soon publicised in all the newspapers. The company's share price collapsed and the damage done to the brand was so great that the company had to be renamed as Signet! The loss of confidence in Ratners was so great that Gerald Ratner had to leave the company. Brands, it seems, are fragile things. (Although interestingly Ratner returned in 2002 to launch an online jewelley retailer; it will be interesting to see how long customers' memories are.)

Summary points

▸ brands make it easier for us to choose between products – this speeds up the search and selection process

▸ brands allow us to identify with their values

▸ brands are increasingly important on the internet, where it is so easy for anyone to set up that consumers are uncertain of who to trust

▸ brands can lose their charm; even when you think you have won the customers' confidence you cannot relax

▸ brands can make a comeback – think Lucozade, think Tango

▸ brands can become too powerful and dominate too many areas of our lives

THINK about it!

Listed below are some famous brands which compete in the same markets. Imagine each of the brands is a person. Write down four words you would associate with each one in the table below. This may be related to its personality, its physique, its job, its interests and so on. Compare your findings. How might this influence the marketing of the brand?

- Coca Cola
- Pepsi
- Microsoft Xbox
- Sony PlayStation
- Ford
- Peugeot
- Manchester United FC
- Liverpool FC

References

1. Hugh Davidson *Even More Offensive Marketing* (Penguin, 1997)
2. Naomi Klein *No Logo* (Flamingo, 2001)

Finance

The finance department

Close your eyes and picture someone working in the finance department. What do you see? Elderly men hidden away in a back room tapping away at their calculators? Or powerful thrusting executives striding into the boardroom to announce they've just won the takeover bid of ABC Corporation? Either way you may be right. So what exactly does the finance department do?

Obviously, it looks after the money. It helps a firm raise the finance it needs by deciding on the best source of funds and making the relevant arrangements. It monitors what is being spent and what is being earned within the business. And it also advises managers on which projects are most likely to be financially successful.

Finance activities can be divided into two categories:

- **financial accounting** – this involves record-keeping. These people produce financial statements which show the position of the business, such as the balance sheet, and profit and loss statement (see page 108)
- **management accounting** – these activities provide managers with the information needed to make decisions, eg whether there is sufficient cash to do a particular project, whether it is profitable and so on

The flow of money around the business

A business is a system. It takes inputs, transforms them in some way, produces goods and services, and then sells these on. To do this successfully, firms must manage their cashflow very carefully.

The problem is that there are often major differences between the timing of payments. Imagine you own a construction company. You spot a brilliant opportunity, developing the docks in London. This will involve buying the land, building the properties and eventually renting them out. Just imagine how much you are going to spend on land, contractors, equipment, materials and labour, and how long it is likely to be before you actually get any money coming in. This could be a brilliant opportunity to make your fortune, provided you can hang in there long enough and have the cash to survive the short term. Unfortunately, many firms find they can't hold on long enough and are liquidated even though the basic project is sound. This happened with the developments at Canary Wharf in London, where the cash was too slow to arrive. Managing the finance therefore includes estimating cash outflows and inflows, and trying to make appropriate arrangements to make sure the firm does not end up illiquid.

CASHFLOW

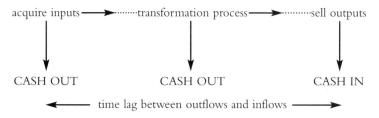

acquire inputs ⟶ ⋯⋯transformation process ⟶ ⋯⋯sell outputs

CASH OUT   CASH OUT   CASH IN

⟵ time lag between outflows and inflows ⟶

Budgets

Budgets are one way that firms use to try and control their cashflow situation. A budget is a financial target that can be set for revenues or expenditure. The target should guide managers in their decision-making. It also motivates because they have something to aim for. From a firm's perspective it means it can plan ahead financially (assuming the budgets are hit).

The value of budgeting naturally depends on how the budgets are set, and whether they are achieved. If a ridiculous number is just dreamt up by an over-ambitious boss, and everyone knows the company has no chance of achieving it, then this exercise is just a waste of time. The best way to set the targets is to discuss them with the people who are going to have to achieve them. If you simply impose them on staff, they are unlikely to feel any ownership of them – and this may mean they do not work particularly hard to make sure they are hit. This does not mean the budgeting process is necessarily easy or comfortable – all managers will naturally want to fight hard to get whatever resources they can, and there can be conflicting views of what is or is not needed to achieve a particular aim.

Budgets are used in very different ways within organisations and are often perceived differently by staff. In some firms budgets are part of the command-and-control mentality; you impose budgets to make sure your staff do not overspend. In other firms, the process is more two-way and it is seen as part of empowerment. Once the budget is fixed it is up to the manager to achieve the targets however he or she wants. The goal is agreed; the method is delegated.

Budgets can, however, be dangerous, which is why some organisations tend to avoid them. If you have set financial targets then your life may become totally dominated by these. Along comes a brilliant market opportunity that could bring huge returns, but you turn your back on it because it will take you slightly over your target, and this would hurt you when it came to appraisal time. Another danger is that you are determined to use up all this year's budget to make sure you get at least the same next year. This is why you'll sometimes find all sorts of unusual expenditure going on towards the end of the financial year, when managers are desperately trying to use up their spending budgets!

Raising the money

If your company needs to raise some money quickly, there are two sources of finance: internal or external.

Internal sources include:
- selling assets, eg, selling your stocks or land
- chasing up the money you are owed (debtors)
- using retained profits.

External sources include:
- selling more shares
- overdrafts
- loans
- creditors (buying items on credit and paying later)
- venture capital.

Before deciding on the best way of raising money, you need to establish how urgent it is that you get the money, and how long are you will need it for. If you need the money for the short term, for example, an overdraft might be more suitable than a loan. Loans are organised over a fixed period of time and paid back in instalments. Similarly, a share issue (which would involve having the documents offering the shares for sale legally checked, taking advice about when to sell them and for how much, and getting permission from existing shareholders to go ahead) would not be suitable if you only needed some money temporarily.

Another consideration when raising finance is the impact on the control of the business. If the existing owners want to retain control of the organisation then they are unlikely to want to sell more shares, as this would bring in other investors. A loan might be more appropriate. However, your ability to get further borrowings might depend on how much has come from this source already. If you have high levels of debt already banks may be concerned about lending you more. The decision about which form of finance to adopt is therefore a combination of factors, such as:
- control
- availability
- amount and the length of time it is likely to be needed.

Summary points

▶ management accounting focuses on providing financial information for managers to make decisions; it is forward looking

▶ financial accounting focuses on financial reporting and is backward looking

▶ managing the money involves timing the inflows and outflows around the business

▶ budgeting sets financial targets

▶ the value of budgets depends on how they are set

▶ the finance needed by the business may be from internal or external sources

Is management accounting more important than financial accounting?

What is profit?

Profit is something that managers strive for, investors dream of and the taxman wants to get hold of. But what is it? And why do we want it? For many people profit is the same as cash. High profit means piles of cash sitting around ready to be spent. A profitable company has millions in the bank. Wrong!

Profit is a technical term and needs to be treated with all the respect that this deserves. It is calculated by using the equation: revenue minus costs. But what do we mean by the term 'revenue'? It is not, as many think, the amount of cash a firm receives from its sales – it is simply the *value* of those sales. So here we have an immediate difference between revenue and cash. If, for example, you sell your products on credit, this counts as a sale (and therefore revenue) even though the cash may not turn up for months. You can have revenue, therefore, and yet not have the cash to go with it.

And what about 'costs'? Here we have even more fun and games. The term 'costs' means the value of what has been used up to produce and market the items that have been sold. If you buy materials and use them up, they are costs; if you don't use them up they are not costs – they are counted as assets because you still own them. Imagine a situation where you bought £100,000 of materials, used up 25% of these and sold them on for £40,000 on credit. In terms of the cash you have spent a lot of money (£100,000) and received none – your bank manager is probably on the phone asking you what you think you are doing. But in terms of profit, the value of your sales is £40,000 and the costs of materials actually used up is only £25,000 – you have a profit of £15,000.

Can you have cash and not profit?

The answer is 'yes'. The internet bookseller amazon.com did not manage to make a profit until 2002 (eight years after it was set up), despite becoming an extremely well-known brand. Establishing the brand and its distribution network meant the firm was not able to cover its costs with its revenue. However, because it offered good returns in the future, it did manage to attract investors and loans from banks. The result was that it had high cash levels but these were generated by means other than its trading profit.

Too much cash

Believe it or not, it is possible to have too much cash! Although the idea of bathing in cash may seem attractive, it is actually quite wasteful – money sitting idle has an opportunity cost. It could be being used elsewhere to earn a return.

Too little cash – how to boost your cashflow

Too little cash is also a problem – as you would expect! Without cash you may well be illiquid. Your creditors may become irritated by your delay in paying and if necessary seek the help of the courts. So what can you do to boost your cashflow?

- You can offload your stock for cash even if it means dropping your prices. Many firms find they need to sacrifice profit at some point to generate sufficient cashflow.
- You could try and 'encourage' the people who owe you money (these are called debtors) to pay up.
- You could encourage cash sales from now on (either by insisting on it or by giving preferential rates for cash payment).
- You could use a debt factor. These are firms that take over your debtors; when you sell something the debt factor pays you and then waits for the customer to pay it (in return for this service it charges interest).
- You could borrow money (if you can convince the bank to lend to you).

Which matters the most, cash or the profit?

In terms of the day-to-day survival of the business, cash is a priority. There is no point telling the bank or your suppliers that technically you have made a profit if you cannot actually pay your bills. To make sure the balance at any moment is at an appropriate level, you may want to produce a cashflow forecast that sets out the expected inflows and outflows over time. Of course, these predictions may not be entirely accurate, but they can at least help to identify any particularly troublesome points and hopefully you can take appropriate action in time.

Following the major downturn in the airline industry after the terrorist attacks of 11 September 2001 in the USA, British Airways axed over 5000 jobs within less than two weeks. It also cut capacity by 10%. Rod Eddington, BA Chief Executive, said at the time 'Cash is king, we must husband cash with great determination … we are looking very hard at anything that takes cash out of the business'. As a result, spending on new capital projects was suspended, there was a halt in buying computer software and hardware, and advertising and promotion were almost halted. The company also began a review of its terms and conditions with suppliers. Faced with a collapse in demand, ensuring the company had enough cash was essential to day-to-day survival.

In the long run, however, there is no point simply having a good cash flow. What you need is to produce something where the value of what you are selling exceeds the value of the items used up, ie, you need to be generating a profit (assuming you are not a non-profit organisation). The greater the profit, the more value you are adding to your basic costs. So cash is important for survival; profit is important to be successful long term.

Is profit a good indicator of success?

Ask most people why they want to go into business, and the answer is ikely to be 'to make profit', but arguably profit is not a particularly good indicator of business success. Most plcs set out to achieve in a whole range of different objectives. Financial performance might be important, but so are social and environmental targets. Visit the Shell website (www.shell.com), for example, and you'll see the company report back on how it has achieved in terms of many different criteria: profits, safety, emissions, employee representation, education and so on. Measuring profit only begins to touch on what the managers believe is important. The Body Shop Mission Statement includes the following:

'To dedicate our business to the pursuit of social and environmental change.

To courageously ensure that our business is ecologically sustainable: meeting the needs of the present without compromising the future.

To meaningfully contribute to local, national and international communities in which we trade, by adopting a code of conduct which ensures care, honesty, fairness and respect.'

Of course profit does matter – we need it to finance expansion and reward investors – but its value must be considered in the context of the overall goals of the organisation. And in many cases, profit is of very limited value as a means of measuring performance – consider a sports club, the government, a community centre, schools and libraries.

Summary points

▶ cash and profit are not necessarily the same

▶ in the short term, cash may be the priority to ensure liquidity

▶ profit may be important to firms, but it's not the only thing they want to achieve

Identify three indicators you might use to measure the success of the following organisations: Sixth Form College, prison, charity, library, restaurant.

Can you trust the figures?

Each year public limited companies must produce a set of accounts for their investors. These are also available to the public. These accounts will include a balance sheet, and a profit and loss statement. The balance sheet sets out what a firm owns at a particular moment in time: it lists the assets of a firm and details how these were financed (ie where the money came from to acquire the assets the firm owns). The profit and loss statement shows the revenue and costs of the firm over the financial year.

Both the balance sheet and the profit and loss are needed to get a good insight into the business. Imagine a firm that has been trading for many years but is going through a difficult patch. The firm may have many assets (eg property and buildings) that it has acquired over the years, even though this year's profits may be low. By comparison, a new but highly successful business may have high profits but relatively few assets (because it has not had long to acquire them). So only by looking at both the balance sheet and the profit and loss do we get a true overview.

Balancing the books

Methods of getting the numbers to say what you want include:

- Depreciation policies: whenever an asset is acquired, it is listed on the balance sheet as an asset. Over time as the asset is 'used up', it is depreciated. The amount it is used up in any one year reduces the value of the asset and is listed as a cost. The problem is that no one is entirely sure how long an asset will last or what it will be worth at the end. Therefore it is very difficult to estimate the cost per year.
- Valuing intangibles: the rules on this vary from country to country, but in some places it is possible to value your brands and include these as assets. This boosts the book value of your company. However, there is no agreed way of doing this; we all accept that the Sony or Intel brands are worth something, but how much? If there is no agreed way, this leaves the door open to creative accounting.
- Sale and leaseback: if your cash looks low why not sell some of your assets and lease them back? This will bring an immediate inflow of cash. In the long term it may increase your costs to lease the asset, but it solves a short-term problem.

In some cases the numbers may be misleading simply because of the way they were recorded. In 2001, Non League Media, a football magazines publisher, had to suspend trading when the group discovered that it had overstated the amount of cash it had on its balance sheet and that there was a corresponding understatement of debtors at 30 December 2000. How did this happen? £292,000 had been wrongly entered as cash when it should have been debtors (ie money still owed to the firm).

When analysing published accounts, you also need to remember:

- The figures are often for a particular moment in time. The balance sheet shows you the firm's assets on a specific day. This may not be very representative of a typical day for the firm. The company is almost bound to choose a day when things look pretty good.
- Accounts only show things that can be quantified and measured in monetary terms. They won't directly reveal the motivation of the staff, the future plans of the management, new products the firm has in the pipeline. Financial accounts also ignore the environmental and social impact of the firm's activities.

The role of the auditors

According to UK law, all companies must not only produce annual sets of accounts; these must also be checked by independent accountants called 'auditors'. The auditors must sign off the accounts, stating whether or not they represent a 'true and fair view' of the firm's financial position.

However, even if the accounts are passed by the auditors this is no guarantee that all is well. In 1996, for example, Andersen's audit reports of Waste Management were found to be misleading and Andersen was fined $7 m. It was discovered that Andersen had not realised that the company's statements overstated its income by more than $1 bn from 1992 to 1996.

In 2001, Andersen was also investigated over its auditing of Enron, a huge US company, which had reported its accounts in such a way as to mislead its shareholders very significantly. This was later described as 'aggressive accounting'. Debt had been hidden and Enron had estimated future profits from deals and put these as current earnings! Enron had to restate all its annual financial statements from 1997 to 2000, resulting in a cumulative reduction in its profits of $591 m and an increase in its debt of $628 m.

Other famous examples of misreporting which had disastrous effects include:

- Polly Peck – this was an apparently succesful fruit-trading business that collapsed in 1990, having hidden away its foreign currency losses in its notes to its accounts. Asil Nadir, the Chief Executive, managed to report huge profits but only by ignoring its losses overseas! Eventually the truth came out and Nadir fled.
- Ferranti International, a major defence business, bought International Signal and Control (ISC), an American company, for £420 m, only to discover that many of its supposed contracts did not exist and the company was almost worthless. Ferranti was ruined.

Summary points

> ▶ profit figures can be made to look good using creative accounting.

> ▶ even audited accounts can be wrong

This year's figures look like they are going to be pretty poor. You have to face the shareholders at the Annual General Meeting in two months' time. A friend has recommended an accountant who could window-dress the figures and make the numbers look a bit better. Do you agree to let the friend have a go at window-dressing your accounts? What would your decision depend on?

Ratio analysis

If you want to assess the financial position of a business, it is common to use financial ratios to place the numbers in some sort of context. You usually have to rely on the figures published in their accounts, but you must heed several warnings:

- these may be several months out of date and so are no longer relevant
- any published figures will almost certainly have been manipulated to create a favourable impression, they only show a position on a particular day – this may not be the 'normal' picture.

Terry Smith, who, in his book *Accounting for Growth*, blew the whistle on many of the accounting practices of well-known firms to make their accounts look particularly good, suggested that you read company accounts back to front. Whatever they don't want you to see will be at the back, so maybe you should start there.

ROCE

One of the most important ratios is known as 'return on capital employed' (ROCE). If you are considering putting money in the bank, betting on a horse or lending someone money, you are naturally interested in how much you have to invest, and how much is the profit, in relation to this initial investment. Capital employed is the total money raised from loans, issued shares and the company's retained profits. ROCE measures the return on this investment. If you are assessing a firm purely in financial terms, the bigger the ROCE the better. The ROCE of a firm should be compared with its competitors and other investment opportunities (taking account of the risk involved).

The acid test

A second key ratio is known as the acid test. This assesses the liquidity position of a business, ie whether it has sufficient funds readily available to pay off its short-term debts. This ratio is measured by:

$$\frac{\text{current assets without stock}}{\text{current liabilities}}$$

The current assets include the firm's debtors (money owed to the business by other firms) and its cash (money which the firm has in the bank). Stocks are not included in this ratio because they are regarded as the least liquid of the firm's current assets (these might be hard to sell if, for example, market conditions change). The acid test is therefore a tough test of liquidity because it does not count the things you usually expect to be selling to bring in more money.

Typically, the acid test ratio has a value of about 0.8. This means that even when ignoring stocks, a firm has enough short-term assets to cover 80% of what it has to pay out over the next 12 months. Given that the stock is likely to make up for at least the other 20%, the firm should be perfectly liquid at this level. However, you do need to adjust the ratio for the context – if the figure was a bit lower for a successful supermarket, this may not be a matter for concern because its stocks can almost certainly make up the difference.

If, however, the acid test is very low you might be concerned. This would mean the business may have problems paying its bills. So the acid test needs to be high enough to ensure the bills can be paid; but you don't want it too high because this may imply:

- the amount owed to the firm by debtors is too high (in which case you need to be careful that you will actually get paid)
- the cash is too high (cash is good but it could be earning better returns elsewhere).

It is important to look at the ROCE and the acid test combined. Some firms are very profitable but manage their cashflows badly and so are liquidated because they do not have the money they need when they need it. You need to check on this with the acid test ratio. Equally there may be firms which manage the timings of their payments and receipts of cash very effectively but do not actually manage to generate a profit. A successful firm, however, will be liquid *and* profitable.

Gearing

A third crucial ratio is called gearing. This looks at a firm's long-term sources of finance and measures how much of it is borrowed. High gearing means that a high proportion of its funds are borrowed. This is measured by:

$$\frac{\text{long term liabilities}}{\text{capital employed}} \times 100$$

High gearing may be a matter of concern because of the interest payments. In an unsuccessful year, a firm may struggle to pay its interest if it is highly geared. On the other hand, whether high gearing is a problem will obviously depend on the rate of interest being paid. And it is important to remember that if firms did not borrow this would severely limit the number of projects they could undertake.

Dividend yield and the PE ratio

The ROCE, acid test and gearing give a good insight into whether the business is profitable, whether it is liquid and its present level of borrowing.

As an investor, you are particularly interested in the returns you get from your investment. This means you are likely to focus on the dividends (ie the amount paid out by the company to its shareholders) and changes in the share price. The dividend paid by the company on each share may be compared to the present share price; eg, if the dividend is 5 pence and the share price is 50 pence, this is a 10% return. This is known as the dividend yield.

Secondly, an investor will be interested in the level of present share price – is it too high or not? The share price is often related to the earnings per share of the company (this is known as the price earnings (PE) ratio). The earnings per share are simply the profits of business divided by the number of shares – it shows how much the firm could have paid out per share if it had given out all its profits. If the PE ratio is high, this indicates that investors are willing to pay relatively high prices compared to the company's latest profits; this suggests there is a confidence in the company. If the PE ratio is low, this means the price being paid is very low compared to the company's profits.

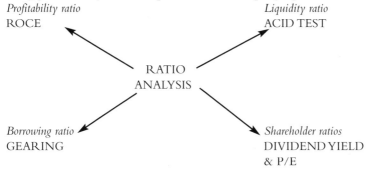

Profitability ratio
ROCE

Liquidity ratio
ACID TEST

RATIO
ANALYSIS

Borrowing ratio
GEARING

Shareholder ratios
DIVIDEND YIELD
& P/E

Summary points

- ratios help analysts make sense of the accounts

- different ratios analyse different aspects of a firm's financial performance

- ROCE looks at a firm's profitability; gearing looks at its long-term lending; acid test looks at liquidity; dividend yield and price earnings are shareholder ratios

Which of the two companies below would you invest in? Why?

Ratio	Company A	Company B
ROCE	25%	18%
Gearing	60%	45%
Acid test	0.8	0.9
Price earnings	8	20

Human Resource Management

What is Human Resource Management?

The Human Resource Management (HRM) function is responsible for the management of people within the organisation. This involves many different activities including:

- the recruitment of new staff
- training
- assessment (appraisal)
- career development
- employee participation
- rewarding staff.

These activities can be categorised in terms of:

- creating an effective workforce (eg recruitment and selection)
- developing a suitably qualified workforce (eg assessment of staff; training and development)
- maintaining an effective workforce (eg developing a reward system; improving employer–employee relations).

The objective of HRM is to ensure the organisation has the people it needs to achieve its objectives. This involves the right number of people, with the right skills and right attitudes. The aim of HRM is not to make people happy – it is to ensure that they are managed in such a way as to maximise their contribution. As its name suggests, HRM regards people as a resource that has to be managed in the same way as any other resource – i.e., care has to be taken about how people are selected, how they are maintained and used. Imagine you employ someone on a reward package of £30,000 a year; if they stay 10 years then even ignoring pay increases this represents an investment of £300,000. If you think of the care which managers take when spending this amount of money on a new machine, the idea that we invest this into a person based on one or two relatively brief interviews is quite incredible; particularly when evidence suggests that the interview process is haphazard to say the least.

While appreciating the importance of recruitment and selection, HRM also recognises that there is no point spending time and money on these areas if you then leave people to themselves and fail to manage them properly once they are employed. People need to have direction; they need to be clear of the objectives of the organisation. They need to be motivated, coordinated and inspired.

Different approaches to HRM

The way in which HRM is approached is likely to differ significantly between firms. These differences vary between 'soft' and 'hard' HRM.

Soft HRM focuses on the human side. It regards people as important and wants to involve them in decision-making. Participation and listening are regarded as important. According to 'soft' HRM:
- employees are assets
- effective employer–employee relations are vital and involve two-way communication
- employee involvement counts.

Soft HRM is built around McGregor's Theory Y[1]. This describes managers who believe that:
- work is as natural as play for employees
- individuals want to contribute
- individuals can be creative given the right incentives.

In contrast, hard HRM puts more emphasis on the management side of things, and tends to assume the managers know best: 'We are willing to listen but ultimately we know what we want and what is best for the employees'. According to 'hard' HRM:
- managers know best
- employees are a necessary cost
- efficiency is the key to managing people.

Hard HRM is built around McGregor's Theory X, which describes managers who believe that:
- employees do not naturally like work
- employees need to be controlled and coerced.

As well as differing in their overall approach to people, organisations will also differ in the way they deal with specific aspects of HRM. Take recruitment and career development: Coca Cola typically hires university graduates with little or no industry experience and trains them up. The company sets out to instil its relatively raw recruits with the corporate values and the knowledge they need. It tends to offer fairly secure jobs and promotes heavily from within. Pepsi, by comparison, seeks to hire people with more experience and from a wider range of backgrounds. Pepsi encourages and indeed seeks individualism much more than Coca Cola.

The responsibility for HRM activities also varies between organisations. In small firms there are unlikely to be HRM specialists. HRM activities are likely to be seen as the part of the senior managers' job. As organisations grow they are more likely to appoint HRM specialists, although this depends on the values of the owners and the senior managers.

Even if there is an HRM department within an organisation, the trend has been to delegate more activities to the functional managers (eg marketing, finance and operations) as part of their jobs. Increasingly the departmental managers or team leaders are expected to manage the human resource issues within their own area themselves. The HRM department will provide advice and specialist services but the actual day-to-day management is the province of others.

HRM and the external environment

Like all aspects of business decision-making, HRM is affected by the external environment. Staff must be recruited from the available labour pool; the rewards offered must fit with the current expectations of those in the labour market; the way in which staff are treated must fit with the values of employees and the current legislation. In the UK, for example, the minimum wage is a relatively new phenomenon; there is also much greater protection for employees in terms of the maximum hours they have to work and the amount of time allowed for maternity leave as a result of recent legislation.

Trade unions

The trade unions represent an importance force within the HRM environment. Unions are organisations which represent employees. In the UK the history of unions and management has often been one of conflict. In the 1970s this was particularly evident, with managers and unions often fighting over how to divide the 'profit cake'. The Conservatives were elected to power in 1979 partly on a ticket of reducing union power, which they set out to do with various employment acts. Organising an official strike became a much slower process, the financial consequences for a union of having an unofficial strike became much more severe and the way in which unions could protest was restricted. Since then union membership has tended to decline (although there are still nearly 8 m union members), but the relation between unions and managers has generally improved. There is now a greater sense of partnership, with both sides working towards the same aim. If the business wins, employees and owners can both win as well. If the business struggles then there is less for everyone; the issue is not how to divide the cake so much as make the whole cake bigger.

However, the level of employee involvement in the UK remains very different from other countries. In Germany, for example, a two-tier board system is common. There is a Board of Directors just as in the UK, but there is also a board with employee representatives. There is much a greater sense of cooperation between employers and unions because it is embedded in the culture. The principle of co-determination (ie that the future of the business should be determined by managers and employees) is widely acknowledged in Germany.

The work–life balance

Among the many human resource issues in the external environment, one of the major ones facing firms at the moment is the increasing demands from employees for a better work–life balance. More people now expect to be able to build their work around their own circumstances – they want to work to live, not live to work. This means that, for example, they want more leisure time, greater flexibility over the hours worked and more childcare provision. As S. Friedman[2] and others have highlighted, the world of work is very different from that faced by previous generations. In America, for example, he highlights that:

- women now make up 48% of the workforce
- 40% of all workers are members of dual-earner couples
- 60% of married women workers have children under six years old
- 23% of employees are single parents
- a growing proportion of families have responsibility for the care of elderly relatives
- the working day for professionals is often nine hours or more.

An increasing proportion of the workforce is therefore trying to balance work and home. The stereotypical male breadwinner who went out to work whilst the wife stayed at home has long since disappeared. If firms are to hold on to their employees and to keep their staff committed, they have to think creatively of ways to help people to maintain a career whilst also dealing with issues in their own home lives. At the same time, organisations must consider their own objectives and see if they can accommodate staff needs as well as their own.

Interestingly, legislation is already reflecting these changes in the workplace. In the UK, for example, new legislation will require employers to seriously consider requests from employees to work part time or to work from home. Although there may be reasons to reject such requests (eg if it prevents the firm meeting its demand or imposes a major cost burden), the emphasis will shift towards the employer taking such requests much more seriously than in the past.

ageing population   more people wanting to work from home

HUMAN RESOURCE MANAGEMENT
AND THE EXTERNAL ENVIRONMENT

more educated workforce

new technologies
requiring new skills   trade union membership decline

changing legal environment

Changing patterns, changing skills

A further development in the world of work in the West has been the decline of the primary and secondary sectors of the economy. This has been accompanied by the rise of the knowledge worker. Employees such as consultants, engineers, teachers, surgeons, analysts and accountants are hired for their ideas, their experience and their insight into problems, rather than any ability to physically make anything. Such people are likely to be attached to their profession more than to any one organisation – they see themselves first and foremost as lawyers, advisers, consultants rather than employees of company X or Y, so corporate loyalty may be difficult to build. If they leave the business they take their knowledge with them, so retaining staff is a key issue. So is training; knowledge needs to be updated and refreshed to keep relevant – it is not like having a skill for life.

Summary points

- HRM involves managing people at work to help the organisation achieve its overall objectives

- soft HRM focuses on *people*

- hard HRM focuses on *management*

- the activities of HRM will be affected by the environment in which the firm operates

- the HRM environment will differ from country to country

- changes in the HRM environment include greater demands for a better work–life balance, greater emphasis on knowledge, more women working, more part-time work

Managing your people

Managing Directors all over the globe readily say that the 'people in our organisation are its greatest asset'. John Sutherland, the Chief Executive of Cadbury Schweppes, said, 'Creating value is 20% about the numbers and 80% about people because people create value. People are our business.' It's certainly true that a firm's employees can make the difference between success and failure. The employees are the ones who innovate, who come up with new and better ways of doing things, who provide a smile for the customer, who get things done. They are the ones who plan, who organise, who find solutions. You can imitate a product relatively easily, but you can't copy the imagination and creativity of a competitor's staff. Good management means getting the right people, training them properly, motivating them and unleashing their talents. But what often happens is that bad management leads to apathy, disinterest and de-motivation. And the result? People work at half-pace, they look for reasons not to do things rather than finding ways of solving problems, they don't care about quality and they definitely don't care about the customers.

Organisational structure

Organisational structure is particularly important in the effective management of people, especially as a firm grows. The structure is the backbone of any business. It is the framework into which the people fit and work.

Look at this description by John Kay of Oxford University[3] and you'll appreciate the importance of an appropriate structure (or at least the problems of an inappropriate one!):

'Why doesn't anyone say what they mean or mean what they say?' asked the questioner who had just arrived at Oxford University, having sat through an interminable committee meeting. Oxford remains one of the world's leading academic institutions but it actually has no clear structures of authority, accountability or responsibility: a complex mix of committees with ill-defined and overlapping responsibilities. It lacks any mechanism for making decisions: 'In many cases university decisions are not specifically made at all; they just emerge and it is often difficult to tell at what point a discussion became a decision ... Several devices were used to avoid decisions. The most frequent was simply to avoid raising any potentially contentious issue which was a universal recipe for inaction ... Those who hold university posts have executive titles but no executive authority. They enjoy responsibility without power ... Oxford has nothing that can be recognised as policy, strategy, resource planning or budgeting.' A poor structure combined with a non-commercial culture clearly makes decision-making at the university something of a difficult process!

Structure is not a big issue when a business is small. A few people help each other out and tend to deal with whatever needs to be done between them. As the business grows and more people are involved, it becomes important to organise who does what more closely. Otherwise real problems develop with a lack of clarity of who should be doing what and when. This can be wasteful because jobs are done twice or not at all, or too late to be useful; it can also be demotivating because no one is sure who is supposed to take control of what.

Designing the structure

Designing an appropriate organisational structure involves making decisions about:

- The design of jobs – Should individuals or departments specialise in particular activities or should they be more generalist? Should jobs be narrowly defined so that employees focus on a limited number of tasks?
- Hierarchy – How many different levels of authority should there be in the organisation? Having lots of levels of hierarchy creates opportunities for promotion and usually means each manager has less people to supervise. Take away the levels and the benefit is that the distance between top and bottom is smaller and this can improve communication. This de-layering approach has been common in many businesses in recent years. It has helped to cut costs and hopefully improve communication, but it has also led to redundancies and increased the workload of the employees who are left, often increasing their stress levels.
- Reporting relationships – Who is in charge of who? Who reports to whom? How many people can a manager effectively supervise?
- The organisation of tasks – eg, do we organise jobs according to their function (eg put all the marketing team together), or regionally (all the people in South East region and North West etc), or by product (eg under particular brand or product managers)?

- Centralisation – To what extent should authority be kept at the centre? Centralisation keeps the major decisions in the hands of experienced employees with an overview. However, it may mean the firm lacks sufficient flexibility to local conditions. Marks and Spencer was criticised for developing too centralised an approach, which meant that its stores failed to meet local needs. In the final few months before C&A closed its 109 UK branches in 2000 (after 78 years in the UK), it allowed its local managers to decide what to stock in their own stores. The company had its best performance for years but it was too late to reverse its decision to close up the UK shops.

Forms of organisational structure

There are several different types of organisational structure that are adopted by firms. The most common ones include the functional and divisional forms. The 'functional' approach keeps people with similar technical skills together, such as marketing and finance specialists. This is a very common form of structure that enables people with similar skills to focus on a problem. However, it can lead to a failure to develop an overview of the problem or to appreciate the work and issues of other functions; it can also lead to interdepartmental rivalry.

An approach that is often adopted in this situation is called the divisional form. In this system, activities are organised based around products, geographical areas or customers. While such an approach provides individuals with a clear focus (on their area or product), it can lead to very separate lines of thinking and coordination across the organisation becomes an issue.

Another organisational form is the matrix form in which there are dual lines of authority. This is an attempt to integrate across functional lines. For example, individuals may work on a particular project for example; they are then responsible to the project leader as well as to their own functional leader. The benefit of this approach is that you gain from two (or more) perspectives. Imagine you are teaching first-year marketing at university on a business course. It would be useful to have the input of the whole marketing department with all its experience and skills. At the same time, it would be useful to have the perspective of someone coordinating all of students' first-year courses so you get an understanding of what is being covered elsewhere.

A functional structure

A matrix structure

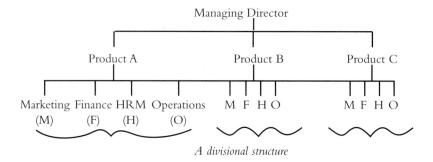

A divisional structure

Increasingly, organisations have been using other firms to supply some of their functions and provide various activities. In schools, for example, the food may be provided by a catering firm, the security by an outside specialist firm and so on. In this case we can talk of a 'network' organisation in which a business concentrates on its areas of core competence and buys in other services. We can even talk of 'virtual organisations' which buy in functions and form teams as and when they are needed (see page 124).

According to Warren Bennis[4], the trend is for organisations to move away from a bureaucratic structure (which involves clear rules and regulations and well-defined roles) towards an 'adhocracy'. This phrase was invented by Alvin Toffler in the 1960s and describes a very flexible organisation which:

- does not consist simply of full-time employees but involves a range of flexible staff including part-timers, temporary staff and subcontractors. This enables a firm to react more effectively to changes in demand conditions, and balance supply and demand more effectively
- has less layers of hierarchy. Many organisations have de-layered in the last 20 years. This is part of a move towards empowering staff. It also cuts costs!
- encourages participation and employee involvement. Modern organisations often recognise the value of employees' ideas and want their input.

Summary points

- ▶ the structure of an organisation can help or hinder an organisation's success

- ▶ structural design involves issues such as the design of jobs, reporting relationships and the degree of centralisation

- ▶ different organisational forms include functional, divisional and matrix structures

- ▶ the organisational structure must change with the nature of the environment and the expectations and skills of those within it

THINK about it!

Look at the organisation you are in at the moment and try to draw its organisational structure. Why do you think it has been organised like this? Do you think this structure works? What changes would you make to it? Why?

Motivating your staff

Motivation is an important element of successful performance. A motivated employee is more likely to turn up, try hard and be concerned about the quality of the work. Motivate your staff and they are more likely to go the extra mile to help the business succeed. As Field Marshall William Slim[5] wrote, 'Morale is a state of mind. It is that intangible force which will move a whole group of men to give their last ounce to achieve something, without counting the cost to themselves; that makes them feel that are part of something greater than themselves'.

So how do we motivate our staff?

Not surprisingly, there have been numerous studies and theories on motivation. The scientific approach believes that people are primarily motivated by money. According to this view, put forward by Frederick Winslow Taylor[6], employees respond to being trained how to do a job and being paid accordingly. Given the right training and tools, employees' productivity increases and they can be paid more as a result. The firm gains from higher output that it can then sell, while employees gain from better pay. This approach has a certain appeal, but it tends to portray individuals as simple economic machines: more money *equals* more effort.

The Human Relations School based on studies by people such as Elton Mayo[7] highlighted the fact that people have social needs as well as financial ones. When they go to work they benefit from working in groups and like to feel needed. Through a series of studies such as the Bank Relay Assembly Room, Mayo found that employees responded very positively when managers showed an interest in what they were doing and asked them about their work.

Herzberg and Maslow

Other motivational theorists include Herzberg[8] and Maslow[9]. Herzberg split potential motivational factors into two groups: hygiene factors and motivator factors. Hygiene factors are things such as basic pay, working conditions, and company rules; if these factors are wrong (pay is too low, the conditions are uncomfortable or the rules are stupid) people are naturally demotivated. If the hygiene factors are put right, people will stop being demotivated; however, these things in themselves do not actually motivate – they simply prevent dissatisfaction. According to Herzberg, motivators are a completely different set of factors, such as greater recognition and greater authority. People respond to challenge in their job, to being told how they are getting on and to greater variety and interest in the work. Managers need to ensure that hygiene factors are in place to prevent dissatisfaction, and then ensure that motivators are there to motivate.

Maslow introduced the concept of a hierarchy of needs, identifying five levels of need we are all supposed to have. At the most basic are physiological needs (such as hunger and thirst), then the need for security (to feel safe), social (the need to belong), esteem (the need to feel respected) and finally self-actualisation (the need to feel fulfilled). To motivate their staff managers must offer people the chance to move on to their next level of needs.

Typical rewards a firm might offer for each level of needs are listed below:
- self actualisation – greater authority
- esteem – a bigger office, a more important-sounding job title, promotion
- social – teamwork, social events, allowing people to be involved
- security – job security, union representation and involvement, pensions
- physiological – basic pay, canteen

Getting it wrong

If you fail to motivate your staff, then don't be surprised if they don't turn up, don't try very hard to get it right and do their best to make life difficult for you. When Railtrack, the firm responsible for the UK railway network, was put into administration in 2001, the low morale of staff was said to pose a threat to safety. One of the causes of this demotivation (apart from the uncertainty about the future of the organisation) was the fact that many employees had seen their own shares collapse in value. On average, staff lost shares worth £1100. Many employees left the business, and these factors contributed to a poorer quality service and even raised possible safety problems.

In 2001, the police force had also reached a low point in terms of morale. This could be seen in the number of working days lost per year. For the police it was an average of 12 days per officer; compare this to an average of 11 days for the health service, eight for school teachers and seven for industry in general.

What about money?

Money certainly helps to pay the bills, buy a meal, arrange a good holiday and give a feeling of security, but is it enough? How powerful a motivator is it? In some ways it is naturally appealing to employers – you give people money and they can decide what to do with it. Unfortunately there are a number of problems in using money to motivate. Firstly, although people often feel good when you first give them more money, they soon take it for granted; the first time your pay cheque increases you celebrate, but you soon become used to the higher pay – if it goes back down again then you are likely to be annoyed, but if it stays where it is, so what? On a day-to-day basis an increase in pay will soon lose its power.

Another problem is that the more you pay someone, the more you will have to increase their pay next time to keep them interested in the work. If you earn £10,000, a £1000 pay increase seems quite a lot; by the time you are earning £80,000 it no longer seems that amazing! But you cannot keep paying all the people more money all of the time, or you won't have a business left.

The combination of these factors naturally forces firms to look for rewards that are longer lasting and more powerful. Of course pay counts – people want status, they want fair rewards for their efforts, they want a comfortable or even an extravagant life. But on a daily basis they also want a stimulating job, and this is where job design counts and where managers can try to meet employees' higher level needs by offering them "motivators". Challenge, variety and the opportunity to make decisions can be far more powerful than a pay increase.

Sir Ernest Shackleton, a famous explorer, put a now famous advert in the newspaper in 1914 for volunteers for his latest Antarctic expedition. It read: 'Men wanted for hazardous journey; small wages, bitter cold, long months of complete darkness, constant danger, safe return doubtful, honour and recognition in case of success'. Anyone responding to this was clearly interested in the challenge, not the money! The advert attracted 5000 people, of whom 27 were selected for one of the toughest expeditions ever experienced.

Summary points

- motivation matters – it can affect the quality of service, staff's productivity and costs

- Herzberg distinguishes between hygiene factors and motivators; some factors prevent dissatisaction (hygiene factors); others motivate (motivators)

- Maslow introduced a hierarchy of needs; this highlights the fact that individuals will have different needs

- money may have an effect on staff, but it is not necessarily the strongest of motivators

You are the Head Teacher of a secondary school. Morale at the school is very low amongst teaching staff and staff want more money. You cannot pay more because the pay bands are decided nationally. What can you do to motivate your teaching staff? Outline the steps you would take over the next few weeks to decide on the best course of action.

Motivation in action: Richer Sounds

Richer Sounds is a hi-fi retailer which was set up by Julian Richer in 1978 and has now become one of the most successful retailing operations in the UK. It has been in the *Guinness Book of Records* for six years, for having the highest sales per square foot in the world. What is the secret of its success? The answer is a complete dedication to customer service, reinforced by an incredibly motivated team. Richer has a clear message: to provide the best quality service for your customers, you need your colleagues (as every employee is called at Richer Sounds) to give 110%. Not that this means they have to work long hours; in fact this is one of the things Julian Richer is adamant about – 'workaholics are no fun', he says in his book *The Richer Way*; if you do your job properly to begin with, you shouldn't have to work long into the night or six days a week. What matters is that you are having fun, that you are thinking of ways to improve the service the customer receives and that you are behaving with integrity at all times.

Reward schemes

When it comes to motivating staff, Julian Richer is a great believer in measuring performance and then recognising and rewarding achievement. Every customer is asked to rate the quality of the service they receive; if a salesperson is rated as 'excellent' they receive a bonus, if they are rated 'poor' they are penalised. Each colleague's rating is regularly measured and their performance discussed. Colleagues are also encouraged to contribute to the suggestions scheme. Every new idea that is submitted is personally read and acknowledged by Julian Richer, and colleagues receive a small reward between £5 and £25 for each suggestion they submit. When the business started Julian calculates that he came up with about 90% of all the ideas within the firm and the colleagues came up with the remaining 10%. Nowadays, thanks to the suggestion scheme, this ratio has been reversed; colleagues submit about 20 ideas per year on average, which is well above the usual rate of suggestions in other schemes. Although the basic pay of the sales team is kept relatively low, they are able to achieve high overall rewards by gaining bonuses for good customer service, for providing suggestions and through their earnings from the company's profit-sharing scheme.

Other rewards for staff include the use of the company's two Bentleys and a Jaguar XJS convertible that are given to the three best performing stores each week to do with as they wish. Colleagues can also make use of the five company holiday homes in the UK and in Paris. There is a well-funded health care scheme and a hardship fund if they have financial difficulties. Loyalty is rewarded: staff who have been with the firm five years join the Five Year Club and are invited to dinner with Julian Richer at a top-class restaurant such as the Connaught, Savoy or Ritz; they also receive a sterling silver lapel pin and are invited to join Julian for a two-day break once a year.

Responsibility, communication, encouragement

Julian Richer maintains very close contact with colleagues, regularly visiting stores, as well as ringing them up to comment on their suggestions and weekly performance. What is particularly important, he feels, is that people are contacted when they have done well, not just when they have made a mistake.

People are encouraged to take on new responsibilities and, as a result, many of the staff have two different jobs; as well as working in the store they might also sit on one of the company's committees. Staff are also responsible for inspecting and monitoring the performance of other stores. Rather than having a separate regional manager to oversee all the shops in a particular area, the company appoints colleagues as associate directors. These associate directors are responsible for one of three areas – merchandising, people or procedures – depending on their own skill. A particularly interesting aspect of this approach is that each store is assessed separately by three different directors – each one focusing on a different aspect of the business instead of having one inspector trying to monitor very different areas. Each associate director is also a store manager, to ensure they fully understand the front-line business, and this dual role system provides colleagues with variety and challenge.

As well as encouraging people to try new jobs, the company also encourages them to admit if it does not work out; unlike most organisations demotion is not unusual or frowned upon. If someone is demoted, he or she is not regarded as a failure – people try new tasks and if it does not work out they move onto other challenges.

This somewhat unusual approach to motivation seems to work (look at the sales figures!), and Julian Richer has been employed by many other companies, such as Asda, to advise them.

Summary points

▶ Julian Richer uses a whole range of devices to persuade staff to focus on customer service and improving the business. He does not rely only on pay – he uses many other forms of incentive

▶ Julian Richer shows an interest – he wants to know how you are doing; this links with Mayo's findings

THINK about it!

Do you think Julian Richer's approach would work in your organisation? Why? Why not?

Employee involvement

An important trend in the last 20 years has been a major shift towards greater employee involvement. The potential of staff to add value to the organisation has increasingly been recognised.

Leading the way: John Lewis Partnership

A UK firm with a particularly strong record of employee involvement is the John Lewis Partnership. As co-owners of the business, all partners (as employees are called) are given the opportunity to have a share in the policy and direction of the organisation. This does not mean that everyone has to vote on every decision or that partners have to agree to everything that managers do, but simply that managers are held accountable to the employees. Managers are expected to lead the business forward; they are expected to take the decisions to make the business profitable and successful. At the same time they know that they will always have to answer for their decisions to their staff; this is because every partner has the right at the appropriate time to question the actions of the managers and to receive frank answers. This has the effect of making managers think very carefully about their actions, and ensures that they always take into account the impact on other partners.

This high level of management accountability leads to much more preparation before any decision is taken, compared to other organisations in the UK. In many ways this style of decision taking is similar to the Japanese management approach: managers take longer preparing the ground, discussing, and gaining acceptance, so that once a decision is taken it can be implemented relatively quickly. John Lewis is especially proud of its weekly journal, *The Gazette*, which is distributed throughout the group. Unlike many company magazines which have little relevance for employees, this is a lively, vibrant publication which stimulates reader interest and promotes discussion of a wide range of business issues. Most unusually, full details are given of the previous week's trading with statistical tables, graphs and regular reports on progress in all areas of the busines. It is a fixed principle that all announcements about the business should appear in *The Gazette* either before or simultaneously with publication in the national media. Although the *Gazette* sometimes gives information away to competitors, the firm believes the gains from openness outweigh the problems. 'Why are some companies much more willing to drop information in the direction of City analysts, than they are to share that same information with their staff who might actually be able to do something constructive with it?' asks Mr Hampson, John Lewis' Chairman.

Empowerment

Empowerment occurs when individuals are given a high degree of control over their working lives. For example, they may be able to agree terms directly with customers without always seeking permission and agreement from above; they may be able to organise their own work schedules and determine what they will be doing at any minute. The idea is that if people control their work, they will be more committed to it.

At the Timpson's stores in the UK, for example, employees are encouraged to solve problems for themselves, and can spend up to £500 dealing with a customer complaint without seeking clearance. The views of the company's Chairman, John Timpson, about his staff are that 'You have to train 'em and trust 'em'.

Why is greater empowerment needed?
- People want greater responsibility.
- Customers want instant decisions and solutions.
- There is a real need to be flexible to local conditions.

Obviously, even in an empowered situation not all decisions will be taken by the employee; it is a question of degree.

Benefits of empowerment

The benefits of empowerment are fairly straightforward to describe. They include:

- better customer service (from a workforce which actually cares about the quality of its service because they have made the relevant decisions)
- faster service – decisions can be taken instantly
- flexibility – the ability to respond to market conditions without waiting for approval from above
- higher morale because employees feel involved in the process. This fits with the work of Herzberg (motivators) and Maslow (self-actualisation).

According to Hackman[10], the typical behaviour of empowered employees includes the following:

- They show an awareness of the goals and strategy of the organisation. They take an interest beyond their functional specialism, paying attention to company publications, press reports and financial and competitive data. They discuss how their work fits in with then company's overall mission.
- They take personal responsibility for the outcomes of their work, showing by their behaviour that they feel responsible for the results of what they do.
- They continually monitor their own performance, looking for indications of quality and showing a concern for how they are doing on all performance dimensions. They correct and improve their performance without being asked to do so.
- They seek additional resources when they do not have what they need to perform well.
- They take initiatives to help people in other areas to improve their performance.

In reality?

In reality, empowerment can lead to chaos. Employees can begin to do their own thing, resulting in an uncoordinated approach. Decisions made in one area may conflict with decisions made in another. Some employees may enjoy making it up as they go along, but others are actually concerned about whether they are doing the right thing – this can reduce morale because these people want more guidance. People may even reject the additional authority – not everyone wants to have more decisions and more responsibility. So if you are going to introduce greater empowerment, don't just thrust it on people (they may see it as exploitation – more work for the same money). Discuss it, discuss the reasons why you want to do it and listen to the response you get.

Summary points

- there is a general move towards greater involvement of staff in decision-making

- employers now talk of empowering employees, ie giving them greater control over their working life

- empowerment can motivate, reduce supervision costs and lead to a better service

- empowerment may not be welcomed by all employees and may lead to resentment and chaos

 **THINK about it!**

Some people believe that the 'empowerment' is actually a form of 'exploitation'. What do you think?

Teams

What is a team?

Teams are formed when a group of people have a common goal and sense of purpose, and hold themselves mutually accountable for what they do. It is not just a collection of people working together – a team has a sense of identity. The members of a team are interdependent, and each one provides an individual skill. To be successful the different skills within the team must blend together effectively. The management writer Meredith Belbin, in *Management Teams: why they succeed or fail*[11], believed that certain combinations of personality types work better than others. He identified nine team roles that should be present for teams to work best (although there may be more than nine people in the actual team).

Belbin's key roles were:
- the **Plant**: this person is creative and imaginative; he/she is able to solve difficult problems but tends to ignore detail
- the **Resource Investigator**: this role has good contacts outside the team (Mr Fix it!); this person explores opportunities, is an extrovert and is enthusiastic. However, he or she tends to lose interest quickly after the initial enthusiasm

- the **Coordinator**: clarifies goals, promotes decision-making, delegates well and is a good chairperson. However, this person can be perceived as manipulative
- the **Shaper**: this person is able to find a way around obstacles; he or she is likely to be challenging and dynamic; he/she has drive but also provokes others and may hurt their feelings
- the **Monitor/Evaluator**: the analyst of the team who can highlight flaws in an argument; he or she may be detached and unemotional BUT may also be overly critical, and lacks the drive and ability to inspire others
- the **Implementer**: sees to practical planning and scheduling; is disciplined, reliable and conservative BUT tends to be somewhat inflexible and slow to respond
- the **Team Worker**: does not take a leading role but supports others by listening and helping; he or she often smooths things over and builds a team spirit BUT may be indecisive in crunch situations
- the **Completer**: ensures the team meets its targets; is painstaking, conscientious, searches out errors and omissions BUT is inclined to worry unduly
- the **Specialist**: has specialist or technical skills BUT may contribute only on a narrow front and tends to dwells on technicalities and loses sight of the big picture.

Good teams are therefore not about a collection of similar people – you need differences to work together as an effective collective whole. A group of "Plants" would be creative but not get anything done. A group of "Team Workers" would get on well but probably lack ideas or action. As Professor Charles Handy[12] says, a good football team is not made up only of strikers.

Benefits of teamwork

Teamwork is very popular nowadays. More firms are adopting it as a standard way of working. Companies are looking to involve staff to a greater extent, and to benefit from their skills. Cell production, quality circles and kaizen groups are all types of teams created within a firm to use teamwork in the workplace.

The benefits of teamwork include:
- improved performance, as seen in higher productivity, greater flexibility and a higher quality of service. Performance is likely to improve because of shared skills and experiences
- higher motivation as staff feel involved (Maslow's social, esteem and self-actualisation needs; Herzberg's motivators)
- commitment as employees feel part of something and can see what others contribute.

But take a group of people, throw them in a room and close the door and you don't necessarily produce a team. For a team to work there must be:

- a commitment to the goal (and this must be a group goal, not an individual one – in the TV programme *Big Brother*, the contestants are ultimately out for themselves)
- a clear understanding of what the team is trying to achieve
- open discussion so that problems are solved
- trust so that the members are willing to work together
- the desire to reach a consensus.

Team development

Teams often take time to evolve and to start working well together. Tuckman[13] identified four stages in team development known as forming, storming, norming and performing:

- in the **forming** stage a new group comes together. At this stage individuals are often wary of each other. People arrive with ideas of how they expect the group to behave and try to focus on the job in hand because they are unsure of the others
- in the **storming** stage, members begin to grow in confidence, air their views and understand the challenges a bit more. Hostility and confusion often appear at this stage
- in the **norming** stage, the group works out how to come together as a successful unit. Members begin to understand each others' strengths and match these to the different aspects of the challenge
- in the **performing** stage, group roles are fully defined and shared. This is when a group really becomes a team.

These stages could last for a matter of hours or months, depending on the members and the conditions.

The downside of teams

While teams may bring benefits, they are not automatically successful. As Professor Handy points out, 'a good team is a great place to be, exciting, stimulating, supportive, successful. A bad team is horrible, a sort of human prison.' With the wrong people, a team can be a disaster. It can be frustrating and irritating because you know it is not working and is failing to be productive.

Problems with teams include:

- teams can develop their own norms and culture that are different from the desired norms of the organisation as a whole
- teams may suffer from 'group think'. Janis[14] described group think as 'a mode of thinking that people engage in when they are deeply involved in a cohesive group, when the members' striving for unanimity overrides

their motivation to realistically appraise alternative courses of action'. Symptoms include: an illusion of invulnerability, rationalisation and self-censorship

■ teams may take riskier positions than they would take on average if working alone (this is called 'risky shift'). Numerous tests have shown that juries as a whole often give tougher sentences than the individual members would have done.

Summary points

▶ the general move toward teamwork fits with the greater involvement of staff in the workplace

▶ teams often offer numerous benefits for the individuals involved and the organisation as a whole

▶ teams don't always work – it depends on the mix of people

▶ effective teams involve a collection of people with different skills and experiences

 **THINK about it!**

Think about the last time you worked in a team. What were you trying to achieve? How did the team perform? Was it better working in a team or on your own? Looking at Belbin's roles, which role would you say you played? Why?

References

1. Douglas McGregor *The Human Side of Enterprise* (Penguin, 1987)
2. S. Friedman 'The Near Future' *The Economist*, November 2001
3. John Kay 'An object lesson in prevarication' *Financial Times*, 22 November 2000
4. Warren Bennis *Leaders: Strategies for taking charge* (Harper business, 1997)
5. Field-Marshall Viscount William Joseph Slim *Defeat into Victory* (Pan, 1999)
6 Frederick Winslow Taylor *The Principles of Scientific Management* (Dover, 1999)
7 J.H. Smith *The significance of Elton Mayo: The Social Problems of an Industrial Civilisation* (Routledge and Kegan Pau, 1975)
8 F. Herzberg *Motivation to Work* (Transaction, 1993)
9. A. Maslow *Motivation and Personality* (Harper and Bros, 1954)
10. J.R. Hackman and G.R. Oldham *Work Redesign* (Addison Wesley, 1980).
11. M. Belbin *Management Teams: Why they succeed or fail* (Butterworth-Heinemann, 1996)
12. Charles B. Handy *Understanding Organisations* 4th Edition (Penguin, 1992)
13. R.W. Tuckman 'Developmental sequence in small groups' *Psychological Bulletin* 58.6 (1965)
14. Irving L. Janis *Groupthink* (Houghton Mifflin, 1982)

Operations management

What is operations management?

Operations management involves the transformation of resources from inputs into outputs. Organisations take inputs such as people, machines, technology, entrepreneurship and materials and turn them into goods and services. Along the way there are by-products and waste materials.

Operations managements must deal with issues such as:

- where to produce (facilities and location decisions)
- how to produce (eg what kind of production system)
- when to produce (scheduling decisions)
- matching production to demand (making sure the firm is able to meet the peaks in demand).

These decisions are closely linked to the other functions. Marketing should identify what customers want and then, in consultation with operations, the firm can decide what is actually feasible. Given that there will be production constraints (such as the firm's capacity and limits to the flexibility of the process), a compromise of some sorts between marketing and operations is almost inevitable. At the same time, human resources will need to work with operations to ensure the right number of employees with the right skills are available when needed; again, there may be constraints such as the number of skilled staff available. Meanwhile, the finance function is needed to raise money for expansion and to monitor costs.

In negotiation with the various functions, a firm must develop an operations strategy that determines the range of products it seeks to produce, the volume of output it wants to be able to produce and the quality levels and cost targets it seeks to achieve.

The effectiveness of operations management may therefore be assessed on the basis of indicators such as:

- cost
- quality and reliability of the product
- volume of production and flexibility in the process
- speed of the service
- level of service provided.

Effective operations management helps the firm deliver the products the customers want at an appropriate time and cost. It can also provide a competitive advantage: the consistency of McDonald's, the creativity of the Eidos software company (creators of Lara Croft), the taste of Scottish whisky producers, the flair of DKNY, the luxury of Lush soaps are all advantages

created by operations management in conjunction with the other functions of a business.

Goods v services

Many aspects of operations management are similar whatever you produce, but there are nevertheless some key differences between producing services and producing goods. For example:

- goods are tangible; services are intangible
- manufacturers of goods usually have a low level of contact with the final customer – the product is generally sold on to intermediaries before they get to the final customers, whereas with services you usually deal direct with the buyer
- if you make goods you can store your output and therefore stockpiles can be accumulated for busy periods; in services, stockpiling is not an option (you cannot store 'lessons' or 'haircuts')
- manufacturing of goods is often automated, whereas services are generally very labour-intensive.

Making for one

From a marketing perspective, the operations process should be organised in such a way as to provide a unique product for every customer. This is called job production. Think of an architect's designs, an artist's painting, one-to-one piano tuition, the London Eye or the Eden project – the incredibly huge conservatories in Cornwall containing plants from all over the world that have become a major tourist attraction in the UK.

However, the economics of this approach do not always add up. Making tailor-made products is naturally expensive compared to mass production. Therefore there is always a degree of trade-off between producing standard products and services (the cans of beans approach) and offering flexibility (the tailor-made suit approach). However, developments in technology have enabled firms to include much more customer choice while still operating in such a way as to standardise many of their activities. This is known as 'mass customisation'.

For example, the computer company Dell offers customers the chance to choose their own monitor, memory board and features etc. The customer designs his or her own personalised individual computer, although at each stage he or she is actually choosing from a limited number of options, eg they are choosing one from five types of monitor. This means that at each stage of production there are relatively few options, but when the different choices are combined, there are a wide range of products. Dell therefore offers tremendous flexibility but not at a prohibitive cost.

Levi's is also able to offer similar flexibility in the production of its jeans. In the late 1990s the company witnessed a decline in its sales; good design and marketing had helped competitors such as Gap to eat away at Levi's market share. Based in cheaper manufacturing locations, many of Levi's competitors were able to offer better value for money. Levi's reacted by closing several of its plants. At the same time it also developed its Original Spin programme to provide jeans that are custom-made for individual customers. Original Spin uses web-based technology and computer-controlled production equipment to implement mass customisation. With the help of a sales assistant, a customer creates the jeans he or she wants by picking from a set number of colours, a number of basic models, several different leg fittings and two types of fly. The customer's waist, rear and inside leg are measured and the order punched into an in-store computer. At the factory these are cut, made and shipped to the customer's home. A fully-stocked Levi store has around 130 pairs of ready to wear jeans; with Original Spin the number of choices leaps to 750!

Most firms try to offer greater flexibility without making lives more difficult for themselves: in DIY stores you can mix and match your paints to come up with whatever personalised colour you want; in the supermarket you can put together your own salads to meet your particular tastes. Operations management is being asked to provide ever greater flexibility to meet the needs of niches more precisely. As the competition heats up there is an increasing need to meet customers' requirements even more closely than before.

Summary points

▶ operations management is responsible for the production of the good or service

▶ operations management controls costs, quality, flexibility, reliability

▶ there is an increasing need for flexibility as competition increases and customers become more demanding; in response to this many firms have adopted a mass customisation approach

THINK about it!

Think about your organisation. Briefly describe the production (or transformation) process. Imagine you are in charge of managing the operations of this organisation. What sorts of decisions do you have to make? What constraints do you face? How can we measure your success?

Production in action: Aston Martin

If your business is very successful, you might want to treat yourself to an Aston Martin, one the most luxurious cars in the world. Models such as the Aston Martin V8 and the Vantage are aimed at the very top end of the luxury and performance car market, and sell for over £150,000 (without extras!). Even so, the waiting list is several months; no doubt due in part to the fact that only around 80 cars are made each year. Every single car is built by hand to meet the exact requirements of each customer. The customer chooses the colours of the body, the trims, the carpets, the dashboard and even who builds the engine. Incredibly, every single car which leaves the factory is tested by a Board Director – this truly is quality control at the highest level. After successful completion of the road tests, the customers' own seats, door trims, carpets, wheels and tyres are fitted.

The emphasis on quality throughout the process is breathtaking – eg each car is paint sprayed by hand 12 times to ensure there is a perfect paint finish. The outside aluminium panels are painstakingly beaten by hand to form the correct shape. Forget any images of automated production lines – this is old-fashioned job production. The factory comprises a group of highly-skilled craftsmen producing hand-made products.

Some of the different elements of the process are quite staggering:
- about £1200 of leather is used inside the cars; this involves about 10 cattle hides per car. UK hides were used in the past, but because UK cows tend to get caught on barbed wire (which ruins the quality of their hides) Scandinavian hides are now used instead; in Scandinavia they tend to use electric fences to keep their cattle in so the hides are less likely to have defects
- the highest grade Wilton carpet is used throughout the car – even in the boot (with leather trim)
- the company manufactures in-house a much greater proportion of its components for its products than any other manufacturer in the UK; this enables it to keep a very close control over quality
- the application of the paint and the hand-finishing between each coat requires nearly 200 hours of work.

In the company's own words, 'Aston Martin promises an exclusive, exhilirating adventure in an individually produced, true British sports car'. No surprise then that it costs so much!

Summary points

▸ Aston Martin produces cars to order – it is highly customer-focused

▸ Aston Martin highlights that price is not the only factor influencing a customer's decision to purchase

THINK about it!

Imagine Aston Martin was asked to extend its brand name to other products. Identify three product categories where it might be appropriate to use the Aston Martin name. Identify three key factors you think the firm would consider before choosing a product category on which to put its brand name.

Lean and mean

One of the most significant developments in operations management in the last 20 years has been the growth of lean production techniques. Lean production focuses on minimising waste by getting rid of wasted time, wasted materials, under-utilised people and so on. This requires a major rethink about the way production is conducted. The move towards lean is pushed by the importance of getting costs down and quality up.

Lean production includes:

- **kaizen**: a process in which everyone is involved in continuous improvement. Achieving competitive advantage may involve major change, or simply doing lots of things a bit better. Jan Carlzon, the chief executive of the airline SAS, for example, claimed: 'We do not seek to be 100 per cent better at anything. We seek to be one per cent better at 100 things.'

- **just–in–time**: the delivery of items just as they are needed, removing the need for stockholding. However, this may put the business at risk. The UK fuel blockades in 2000 highlighted the dependency of British manufacturers on just–in–time and showed up firms' vulnerability if materials cannot be delivered. Dixon's, the electrical retailer, had to suspend home deliveries to ensure it could replenish stocks at its distribution centres. Land Rover even contemplated importing fuel from Ireland.

- **Total Quality Management (TQM)**: an approach in which everyone is involved in trying to achieve zero defects.

- **flexible workforce**: firms are increasingly using temporary or part-time employees. This enables them to increase or decrease their labour input according to demand conditions.
- **cell production**: this occurs where employees work in teams and are responsible for a complete unit of work; this helps to motivate and increase their commitment.
- **Computer Aided Design and Manufacturing** to reduce development times. The Boeing 777 was the first aeroplane to be produced without a physical mock-up being made; it had been designed totally using CAD.

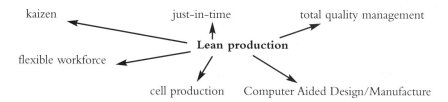

Bow to Toyota

One of the leaders in the field of lean production is Toyota. Toyota has been one of the most efficient and highest quality car producers in the world for many years. The company's flagship factory is at Takaoka and produces 700,000 vehicles a year. On assembly line Number One workers dispatch 800 cars a day along 1.4 km of conveyors and gantries. Each worker has one overriding rule: never send a defective item to the next assembly stage.

Over 4000 temporary workers are deliberately used to provide the company with flexibility in its production process. The company has an intricate network of linked suppliers (called keiretsu) grouped in two enormous organisations: the Kyohokai which has over 200 members and the Eihokia which has over 120 members.

Typically Toyota has a 25% stake in its component makers and adopts a traditionally Japanese paternalistic responsibility for its suppliers and its employees. This commitment includes the unspoken agreement between Toyota and its suppliers that there will be no redundancies. Suppliers may be asked to cut costs but under the Toyota approach they are not allowed to do this by cutting jobs. In the last decade no supplier has closed even though the group's total production has been cut by 25% since its 1990 peak. This close relationship with its suppliers encourages coordinated planning and design so that supplies are delivered in exactly the right quantity, in the right order and at the right time. It is part of a partnership approach with stakeholders which Toyota believes builds long-term success.

Outsourcing and the virtual manufacturer

To be a great manufacturer nowadays does not necessarily mean you have to excel at making things. Many so-called 'manufacturers' oversee a group of other organisations that produce for them. Arm is a UK company which owns the designs for special microchips used in telecommunications equipment, but does not actually make anything itself – the products based on these designs are made by others under licence. This approach of using outside suppliers is called 'outsourcing'. It enables a firm to use other specialist organisations and reduce their own overheads. It provides a business with more flexibility and helps firms to shift some of the risk of a fall in demand on to their own suppliers.

This approach also gives organisations more freedom to concentrate on the areas where they think they have a competitive advantage, such as design, marketing and logistics. Prolion, a leading supplier of robotic milking equipment for farms, outsources assembly and distribution of its machines and even parts of its research and development, while it concentrates on design and customer support.

Similarly, Benetton, which was established in 1965 and is run by three brothers and sisters, has become one of the world's most successful clothing companies by using subcontractors to produce and by selling its products through franchised outlets. Benetton is essentially a virtual manufacturing and distribution system. Rather than directly producing anything itself, the company focuses on building the brand – something it has done extremely successfully. Its advertisements have included images of the death of an AIDS victim, floods in the developing world, a nun and priest kissing, a dead Bosnian soldier and another soldier carrying a Kalashnikov gun. These have generated a great deal of controversy, but most Benetton wearers are under 25 and appear to like the feeling of disapproval. For these customers Benetton represents 'chic rebellion'.

However, sometimes outsourcing production is not suitable because the production process and the firm's production skills are the source of the company's competitive advantage. For example, Zeiss the optical manufacturer produces the world's most expensive lenses which are painstakingly produced using techniques such as ion milling to shape them to accuracies of a hundredth of a millimetre. The manufacturing expertise of the firm distinguishes it from the competition and so it cannot afford to subcontract this part of its operations.

Summary points

▶ lean production involves reducing waste (of people, time, money, machines and materials)

▶ outsourcing enables a firm to focus on its core areas of strength

▶ a manufacturer may be a 'virtual' manufacturer; it coordinates the manufacture and supply without actually producing itself

If Toyota is so good at making cars, does this mean it will automatically be the most successful car company in the world?

Quality, Part 1

The 1980s and 1990s saw the start of a quality revolution. Inspired by the Japanese approach to manufacturing and terrified by their loss in market share, managers in the West finally began to ask themselves, 'What do we actually mean by a quality product or service?' It was a truly momentous day when they realised that quality simply meant meeting customer requirements. As the consumer electronics company Siemens says, 'Quality is when our customers come back and our products don't'.

A quality product does not have to be more expensive than another. It does not have to be the top of the range, it simply has to do what customers expect it to do. When we buy a box of matches we know they won't last forever – we just want them to light easily and safely. If this product does what we expect, we are happy and the firm will have produced a quality product.

So the starting point for any quality operation is the customer – you need to understand what those customers want and expect for the type of product and price range you are aiming to provide.

Previously, quality was defined by removing all the defects that were assumed to be a perfectly natural occurrence when any number of finished products are produced. Quality inspectors did not care about whether the product would sell or not – that was a marketing problem. Quality had nothing to do with producing something customers actually wanted. Provided the finished good had relatively few defects, it was regarded as being excellent quality even if it sat on the shelf unsold for 20 years.

What does the customer want?

If the first rule of quality is to focus on customer requirements, the second is to define what customers want as precisely as possible. What features do they want? When do they want it delivered? What reliability do they expect? What level of service do they expect? The process of quality is about setting and measuring targets.

The third rule of quality is to make sure you ACT on your findings. Agree what needs to be measured (eg wastage rates, delivery times); if the numbers are not right do something about them – take action to bring them around. After all, if the targets are what the customers want, it must be worth achieving them. Quality is exhausting because it requires a complete commitment to setting targets and getting them right every single time. Of course there may be reasons why the targets are not hit, but this is not a reason to let them be missed again. Instead it is a glorious opportunity to find out how to stop it ever going wrong again in the future. A problem is not an excuse, but a new lesson in learning how to bring a process under control. And once the process is under control, you then have to set even more demanding targets to improve quality even further.

McDonald's is perhaps one of the highest quality food providers in the world. Although there might not be a huge variety on the menu and it is not regarded as gourmet cuisine, McDonald's is completely and utterly consistent in its production. The way the items are prepared, cooked and served is the same time and time again, anywhere in the world. Whatever country you happen to be in, your expectations are the same because the company has clearly defined what it wants to achieve, trained the staff and measured whether it happens. This requires a well-organised and systematic approach but leads to superb quality – you buy fast food, prepared appropriately in clean, hygienic surroundings. The company does not sit back but continues to push forward to achieve ever higher standards; there's even a McDonald's hamburger university for the further study of Burgerology!

Summary points

- quality is defined in terms of meeting customer needs
- quality involves setting targets, measuring performance and taking action where necessary ·
- quality is ongoing; if you consistently hit one set of targets, try setting harder targets

- quality begins with the customer not the firm (the customer decides if something is or is not quality); it links to the concept of market orientation

- achieving quality may require something of an obsession!

THINK about it!

Identify three key quality targets you could set in your organisation. Why have you chosen these three? Suggest ways in which quality in these areas could be improved. Identify possible constraints.

A quality guru: W Edwards Deming

One of the leading quality gurus was W Edwards Deming (1900–1993), an American engineer sadly neglected in his early career in his native country. Deming stressed the importance of measurement and improvement but found it difficult to get any managers in the USA to listen. Not so in Japan, where he became a hero. Only much later in his life did the Americans realise the value of what he was saying.

The Deming cycle

The Deming cycle highlights the key elements of quality: it sets out that firms should

Plan→Do→Check→Act

They should plan what they want to achieve, do whatever needs to be done to achieve it, check whether it has been achieved and then act – either taking steps to make sure it happens correctly in future if they failed to get it right this time or, if they have got it right, move the targets up a bit. As Deming said, 'Don't just make it and try to sell it, but redesign it and then again bring the process under control … with ever increasing quality.' A manager once told Deming at one of his conferences, 'I need to know the minimum level of quality necessary to satisfy a customer.' Deming commented, 'So much misunderstanding as conveyed in a few words! The aim, after all, is to keep improving quality and to never be satisfied'.

Deming is also famous for his 14 points of quality. These include the following:

- 'create constancy of purpose toward improvement of product and service with the aim to become competitive and to stay in business and to provide jobs
- cease dependence on inspection to achieve quality. Eliminate the need for inspection on a mass basis by building quality into the product in the first place
- improve constantly and forever every activity in the company to improve quality and productivity and thus constantly decrease costs
- put everybody in the company to work in teams to accomplish the transformation'

This approach to quality is embodied in the European Quality Award ISO 9000 (which used to be called BS 5750 in the UK). To achieve this award firms must set targets, measure the results, keep ongoing records, and take action if the results are not achieved. The award recognises a commitment to the process of quality.

Summary points

- ▶ Deming was a man before his time in the USA. He was not appreciated in the West until US managers saw what he had achieved in Japan

- ▶ Deming highlighted the importance of quality and the need for a systematic approach to improvement. This is now commonly accepted

 **THINK about it!**

Think about the ways in which the quality of your work is assessed. To what extent do you think this system is satisfactory? How could it be improved? What might the constraints be?

Quality, Part 2

Internal and external customers

The quality revolution involves a much broader definition of a customer than was used in the past. We used to think that the customer was simply the person who bought the final product or service. Nowadays a customer is anyone for whom you work, whether this is within or outside of the firm, ie customers can be internal or external. The boss to whom you send reports, the secretary to whom you give work and the shareholders to whom you report are all customers. All of them are expecting something from you and it is your responsibility to provide a quality service.

So do you know what they want? Do you know what they regard as excellent? Do you measure it? Are you achieving it? Do you give the information they need in the correct format? Are you punctual with your work? If not, aren't you preventing others doing their job properly? Do you understand how the quality of your work has an impact on the quality of their work? The quality revolution puts more responsibility on people to think about what they are doing and why they are doing it; it also tries to make people think about how their actions impact on others. British Airways had a huge programme of training in the 1980s in its drive to improve its service, called 'A Day in the Life of'; employees from throughout the company gave presentations on their work so that everyone could understand how all the jobs interrelate to determine the overall success of the business.

The modern approach to quality also empowers people to reject work – if you don't like the work that has been done for you, don't accept it or pass it further down the line. Send it right back to the person who gave it to you and let them deal with it. This is not easy, and demonstrates that achieving quality may require both a shake-up in employer–employee relations and a change in the way people see their role. In particular it is likely to mean an empowerment of staff – they have to be able to check their own work, to be accountable for it and to be willing to reject what they are given if it is not acceptable. This won't work in a traditional command and control system where people just do what they are told to do.

Biting the bullet: Xerox

One of the greatest quality turnarounds in recent years is Xerox. Xerox had once been the market leader in the photocopying market. It had over 90% market share and stood seemingly unchallenged by lesser firms. Then Japanese firms such as Canon started doing what Xerox did but more efficiently and reliably. The Japanese firms also noticed the demand for smaller copiers within firms, whilst Xerox remained convinced that companies would continue to rely on having a few larger copiers for everyone. Xerox was almost wiped out by the Japanese firms, and retired hurt to the corner of the ring.

In the 1990s, however, it re-emerged, and was a much leaner, fitter operation than in the past. It had realised the need to learn and understand what quality really meant. So it undertook a huge programme of benchmarking – it looked at the key drivers of success in its industry and started to measure its own performance against the best in the world. By choosing firms in other industries and not direct competitors, it found allies willing to teach it how and why they excelled at one particular aspect of Xerox's operations – it could be billing, customer relations, delivery or maintenance. Xerox learnt, adapted the ideas and introduced them into its own business along with a major programme of training staff, the introduction of self-running teams and a real focus on meeting internal and external customer targets. The results were dramatic and saved the company.

I'll fix it later

The importance of getting it right first time cannot be stressed enough when discussing quality. It is easy for all of us to think that we'll do what we can and fix any mistakes later. It's certainly how I write books – I write something, and then tidy it up, edit, spell check and so on later. Unfortunately (as my publishers know!) this is a very inefficient way of working and tends to breed complacency – you don't have to think about your work so much in the short term because you are assuming you will have a second go at it. When companies first introduced word processing on a large scale it was predicted that this would lead to a major fall in paper usage. Gone were the days when we used the manual typewriter and when we had to throw the thing away and start all over again if we made a mistake. Now we would get it right on the computer before printing anything off, and the amount of paper used would fall dramatically. How wrong we were! Because we knew we could change things later on we made more mistakes to begin with; we were far more careless than we had been in the past and didn't worry about wasting paper because we could fix it later. Everywhere you go you see this attitude of complacency that builds in errors and wastage.

A genuine approach to quality aims to eradicate this 'fix it later' approach by getting things right first time. This may involve more effort and planning and can certainly be painful to begin with (for example I'd have to learn how to type properly first time), but it saves time and money in the long run because you don't have wastage and errors.

As part of this process of getting it right first time employees are expected to undertake self-checking and focus on a preventative approach. Firms have to stop putting so many resources into teaching people how to deal with a crisis if it occurs and focus instead on stopping it happening to begin with. There is a famous story of a Japanese firm that was asked by an American firm to supply components, and to make sure that there were a maximum of 10 faulty units per 10,000. The Japanese firm sent the components with a separate box of faulty ones. An accompanying letter said they had no idea why the Americans wanted faulty components but they had made them specially! The story highlights the different mind-set of the two firms: the Americans assumed mistakes would occur, the Japanese operated on the basis that there would not be any errors.

Just-in-time

Part of the approach involved in preventing mistakes occurring is known as 'just-in-time' (JIT) production. JIT is an approach to production which does not involve stock levels. Stocks are traditionally kept just in case there is a problem – if there is, you can supply spares. However, under JIT you deliberately lose this safety stock: if there is a problem there really is a problem because you cannot cover for it. This has all sorts of implications: suppliers must be relied on to deliver the right quantity of components exactly when they are required, employees must be trusted because if you have industrial relations problems you have no stocks to sell, and you need a flexible production process which can react suddenly to meet the required demand. JIT also makes it clear to staff and management that they must get it right first time – there cannot be any mistakes because there are no stocks to cover. Also, the fact that once goods are produced they go direct to the customer rather than sitting in a warehouse for ages means that any errors are discovered very quickly and can be traced back to the relevant employees very easily. Once again this puts quality and zero defects at the top of the agenda for all concerned.

Summary points

- anyone you work for (inside and outside the business) is a customer; you should think about what these customers want whenever you undertake a task

- don't fix it later; fix it now and stop it happening again

- you don't need safety stocks; it you get your process right you don't need a buffer

> # ⚠ THINK
> ## about it!
>
> Think about the people you produce work for. Identify
> two internal and two external "customers". What do
> these customers expect from you in terms of your
> work (i.e. what do they look at to decide whether or
> not your performance is satisfactory)? To what extent
> do you think your work meets your customer needs?
> What could you do to meet their needs more
> successfully?

Quality is cheap

Start talking about improving quality to many managing directors and they
turn a little pale. They assume that better quality means better products means
higher costs, because they associate better quality with more expensive inputs
and higher levels of inspection. They haven't embraced the quality revolution.
You don't necessarily need better components to have better quality; you
simply have to make sure that what you are doing meets customer needs and
is less wasteful. And you certainly don't need more inspection; what we are
trying to achieve is more prevention – making sure the mistakes don't happen
at all. Think of it like this and you'll probably realise that better quality can
save you money.

It will cost more on:

- prevention costs such as spending on training, setting up quality circles and
  developing quality systems
- appraisal costs such as inspecting, testing and quality audits,

but it will save money by reducing:

- internal failure costs: scrap, rework, repair, downtime due to problems, the
  cost of holding buffer stock
- external failure costs: liability claims, product recalls, complaints, returned
  goods, lost sales due to quality problems.

Crosby and quality

A great advocate of the cost savings of better quality is Philip Crosby, who
wrote *Quality is Free*[1] in 1979 and *Quality without Tears* in 1984. Crosby believes
that since most companies have organisations and systems that allow (and even
encourage) deviation from what is really required by customers, manufacturing
companies spend around 20% of revenues doing things wrongly, and having to

rework them. Crosby estimates that service companies spend 35% of operating expenses on paying for the consequences of poor quality.

It is up to senior management to lead the way when it comes to improving quality; the employees will then follow their example. Managers must be understanding if mistakes are made, but at the same time must make it clear that the goal is to produce zero defects.

Crosby's 'Quality Improvement Process' (QIP) is based upon his four absolutes of quality:

- quality is defined as conformance to requirements, not as 'goodness' nor 'elegance'. These requirements are determined by customer requirements
- the system for causing quality is prevention, not appraisal (ie it's about preventing mistakes occurring, not fixing them later)
- the performance standard must be Zero Defects, not 'that's close enough'. Aim for the best
- the measurement of quality is the Price of Non-Conformance, not indices (it's not the cost of getting it right you should measure, but the cost of getting it wrong).

Summary points

- quality is cheap; if you get quality right you save money, eg on reworking items or on legal suits

- don't focus on what you spend to improve quality. Focus on what it costs you if you don't

One of your managers has read Crosby's work and has asked you for an extra £200,000 to invest in training. What do you need to know before giving the go-ahead?

Time as a weapon

Close your eyes and dream of a world where you are the only producer of a magic item X that consumers all over the country want. Now wake up and get real. In reality you are likely to have customers who are irritable, fickle and all too ready to dump you for a competitor. You have lots of rivals and are working to tight profit margins. You need to get things done quickly, and deliver what you promised on time (if not earlier!). Saving time wherever you can is important because the old adage is true: 'time *is* money'.

Time is a resource – every hour you wait in a traffic jam is an hour wasted. Every minute when machines are turned off, they are not earning anything. Every second people sit idle, opportunities are being wasted. Every sale lost because your product is not on the market is lost revenue.

Time management

Time needs to be managed like anything else. Effective time management can help to distinguish you in the market place. You wouldn't order from a fast food company such as Domino's Pizza if you had to wait three days for it to arrive. The ability to promise a 24-hour delivery or one-hour photo processing can be a selling point.

The effective use of time may involve:

- critical path analysis – identifying which activities can be undertaken at the same time to cut down on development time; identifying which activities are the critical ones, the ones that must be completed on time or the whole project is delayed (see page 159)
- simultaneous engineering – bringing together designers and engineers to work on a project at the same time rather than have them passing their work from one to another and back again
- effective workforce planning so that you have the people with the right skills and attitudes, and can keep production going
- effective materials planning so the supplies are there on time
- effective use of information technology
- effective management of technology to keep processes as fast as possible.

If you reach the market with a desirable product first, you may be able to get away with a price others only dream of. You may also be able to establish yourself as *the* brand in people's mind. Wrigley's entered the chewing gum market ahead of the rest, and still manages to retain 80% market share. To many consumers, Coca Cola seems the original – the one and only. Of course, being first does not guarantee success, but it may give you a much needed head start.

Summary points

- ⬧ time matters – how long are you willing to wait in a queue?

- ⬧ time is money; every minute waiting is a minute when you are not working

- ⬧ quicker processing and delivery can be used as a marketing advantage

Logistics and supply management

If you talk to a military planner, the importance of logistics is always made clear. There's no point sending your troops into a war zone if you can't keep them fed and supplied. Push on too far and you leave your armies exposed and under-resourced. The same is true in business. Your business units need to be properly served if you want them to do the job you have asked them to do. This underlines the importance of logistics, the process of managing the supplies of parts and the delivery of the final product. It involves organising goods coming in and out of the business. The importance of getting this right is obvious – without the right logistics:
- you may not be able to produce goods because you don't have the supplies
- you may be slow to deliver and so lose customer satisfaction.

To understand the importance of logistics, visit your nearest supermarket and look at where the goods have come from. Wine from France, tea from India, oranges from Spain, cheese from Wales … products from all over the world delivered to your nearest store. Imagine the complexity of getting all of these on your shelves when you want them in good condition, day after day.

The role of logistics

The role of logistics has become especially important with the growth of lean production. Firms do not want to hold buffer stocks (because this ties up money which could be earning interest) and so it is crucial that suppliers are found who can be relied on to deliver the desired goods at the right time. The goods must:

- be of the right quality
- be the right number
- be there exactly on time.

Ideally the goods should also be delivered in exactly the order they are going to be used so there is no need to sort them – they can literally be delivered and used.

Effective logistics management can cut costs, speed up the production time and improve the overall quality of our service. Identifying the right suppliers and building up ongoing relations with them is therefore an extremely important part of operations management.

An important aspect of logistics is the way in which a firm works with its suppliers ('supply chain management'). This area has come under greater scrutiny in recent years because

- consumers are more concerned about issues such as what their products contain, how they are made and the conditions under which they are produced. This means that producers must pay more attention to their supplies because they may be held accountable for them. Companies such as Nike, Gap and Levis, for example, have been attacked for the sweat-shop conditions under which some of their products have been produced
- adding value can begin with the inputs. Many firms have now moved towards using fewer suppliers and building longer-term relationships with them, rather than playing them off against each other. Between 1985 and 1990 Ford reduced the number of its suppliers of components from 2500 to 900. If you always go for the lower price, you may save in the short term but this is unlikely to generate loyalty or cooperation. Greater collaboration with suppliers may include bringing suppliers' representatives into your own plant so they can see the issues involved. In some cases suppliers will even be based in their customers' factories and will take responsibility for the ordering process. This approach was pioneered by the BOSE Corporation, a US manufacturer of home and audio sound systems, in 1987.

For companies such as Wal-Mart, UPS, Ikea and Benetton, effective supply chain management provides them with a significant advantage over the competition. Others often try to learn from them. In a recent edition of *Business Week* it was reported that the US Marines were turning to companies such as Wal-Mart and UPS to help order its supplies. The existing Marine arrangements involve 207 different ordering systems worldwide, most of which are not linked to each other! The aim is to produce a coherent system to ensure that the 173,000 marines can have what they want when they want it.

Logistics and Porter

Behind all business activities is the desire to add value – to sell something that has a greater value than the inputs used to make it. The process of adding value happens throughout the business – it depends on the work of the different functions including people, marketing, finance and operations. Michael Porter[2], a leading US business analyst, developed a model that firms can use to analyse where and how they add value at present, and how they can add more value in future.

secondary activities

Firm infrastructure					Margin
Human resource management					
Technology development					
Procurement					
Inbound logistics	Operations	Outbound logistics	Marketing and sales	Service	Margin

primary activities

This model highlights the various activities within an organisation such as the transformation process (operations), installation and repair (service) and the acquisition of resources (procurement). By analysing these different activities (both primary and secondary) organisations can identify ways of adding more value and creating greater profit margins.

Porter also highlights support activities which are present in each of the primary activities, eg the way in which resources are acquired (procurement), the way technology is used and developed, the way people are managed and the basic systems such as planning and quality control within the firm (the firm's infrastructure).

His model highlights the importance of logistics in his model both at the beginning and end of the value adding process:

- inbound logistics involves the receiving and storage of inputs and the distribution of these to the production process
- outbound logistics focuses on the distribution of products to the customer.

Summary points

- logistics management involves the control of supplies to and deliveries from the organisation

- effective supply chain management can improve the service provided by an organisation

- supply chain management is increasingly important with the demands of lean production and the interest of consumers in how and where a firm's supplies come from

THINK about it!

You are about to have breakfast. Write down the items you will consume and where they were originally produced. This should highlight quite how much is involved to get the products you use and consume on a daily basis from the producer onto your table.

Choosing projects

Management involves taking decisions and taking risks. Managers have limited resources and must choose the best way of utilising these to achieve their objectives. There are, of course, always ways of using money – when have you ever been short of a way of spending? The difficult part is deciding between the different options facing us.

The decision will, in part, depend on a financial assessment of the various projects. This involves undertaking an investment appraisal: considering the amount of money that needs to be raised (and whether it can be raised) and comparing this with the projections of the expected net inflows. Given these figures, a firm can calculate how long it is likely to take to recover its initial investment (known as the 'payback period') and the average rate of return on the investment (which compares the average annual profit with the initial spending). These figures can then be compared between competing projects. A quick payback and a high average rate of return are usually better than a long payback and a low rate of return.

Firms will often have their own investment criteria to help decide whether or not to go ahead with a project. For example, a firm may insist that all projects must have a payback period of less than five years or an average rate of return of more than 20% (or both). The nature of these criteria may depend on the strategy of the firm. A business entering a market with a long-term strategy may be willing to wait longer for a project to payback. Many Japanese firms gained control of the consumer electronics markets by being prepared to gain market share over a very long period.

To assess an investment a firm may also use a method known as 'net present value'. This takes account of the time value of money, ie the fact that money grows over time so the value of future expected inflows is worth less in today's terms. If the interest rate is 10%, £100 in the bank will grow to become £110 in one year's time. Therefore a project that offers £110 in one year's time is only worth £100 in today's terms – this is its *present value*. Similarly, £100 at 10% will grow to become £121 in two years' time; a project offering £121 in two years has a present value of £100 now. By applying discount factors, the present value of all of a project's expected inflows is calculated and compared to the actual cost. If the total present value (ie the worth of all the expected inflows of the project in today's terms) is greater than the cost, the firm is likely to go ahead with the project.

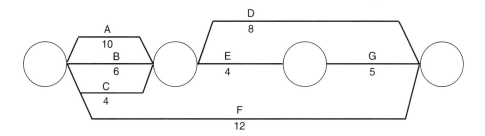

This critical path analysis highlights that several activities can be undertaken simultaneously eg A, B and C. the shortest time in which this project can be completed is 19 days (Activities A, E and G). This is the critical path; if any of these activities are delayed the whole project is delayed. the other activities have float time – they can overrun to some extent without delaying the whole project.

Summary points

▶ projects may be assessed using payback, average rate of return or the present value method

▶ effective investment appraisal depends on the accuracy of the estimates of the future expected inflows

▶ firms set their investment criteria which any new project must hit

You are reaching full capacity at your shoe factory. You are considering investing in a new factory to increase your output. What four things would you need to know before deciding whether to go ahead with the deal?

Project management

Project management is an important element of operations management. It involves organising activities to complete a project as effectively and efficiently as possible. For example, it may involve the development of a new product, the relocation of a business or a new advertising campaign. All of these tasks involve significant sums of money and resources, and so the need to manage them properly is clear. Just think of the difficulties involved in constructing the new Wembley stadium, for example.

The process

The process of project management begins with:

■ an agreement of the different tasks involved. This is likely to involve putting together a project team to gain the experience and views of all the different groups that may be involved in the project

■ an assessment of the duration of each task. This may be easier if the firm has undertaken such tasks before. If they are completely new, the estimates may be inaccurate

■ an agreement on how many resources will be allocated to the project. This will obviously have an impact on the second point. With more money and more people, a firm may be able to reduce the estimated duration of the various tasks

- an agreed definition of success, ie what is required by the end of the project, must be clearly stated. Otherwise people may rush to complete the tasks on time but the quality of the work may suffer
- a system of management. Like anything else, the success of a project will depend on the quality of the management. Simply allocating tasks and estimating durations is meaningless unless people have the skills, abilities and commitment to achieve them.

Project management is therefore about setting clear goals and ensuring that you are kept informed at appropriate stages. It is also about taking action where necessary. It involves putting together a good team of people who have the necessary expertise and abilities, and managing them effectively.

There are, of course, various techniques to help with this sort of challenge. One of these is known as 'network (or critical path) analysis'. This is a process by which the relevant activities are organised in such as way as to minimise the time taken to complete the overall task. Network (or critical path) analysis examines the various elements of a job to identify which ones can be undertaken in parallel, thereby saving time.

Effective project management can help a firm to compete by getting products to the market more quickly (see time management, page 154). It can reduce costs by minimising the waste of resources in coordinating activities effectively and enabling a firm to order supplies only when they are needed, rather than having them arrive too early and having to store them. Poor project management, by comparison, means delays, overruns and a failure to meet promises.

Summary points

- management involves deciding what to do; once the plan has been decided, the project then has to be implemented effectively

- effective project management completes products on time and at a lower cost; this can give firms a competitive advantage

- managing a project properly can ensure resources are not wasted; this can increase the firm's profitability

Your boss has asked you to organise a big party to celebrate the 25th anniversary of the company in six months' time. Some staff (past and present) will be invited, as will major customers and suppliers. In total there will be about 1000 guests.

What other information do you need from your boss before starting to organise the event? Identify the key activities which may be involved in organising such an event. Identify the order in which the various activities must occur (or whether they can be undertaken at the same time as other events). Estimate an approximate time to complete the project.

Innovation

Innovation lies behind many successful organisations. It is the ability to bring new ideas to the marketplace. These ideas might take the form of new products or of new processes. All firms innovate to some extent – they change the way they operate weekly, if not daily. The question is how much they improve, whether this is sustained, whether it is noticeable to the customer and whether this adds value. A company which fails to innovate makes itself a sitting target. Not that innovation simply responds to demand; in some cases it seeks to create it. Just look at the trainers' market (step forward, Nike), and the huge innovation here in terms of design. The innovation in this case drives the demand, pushing people to want the latest.

Innovation is the result of the successful application of research and development (R&D). Spending on R&D is particularly high in industries that rely heavily on new product developments, such as the biotechnology industry. Recent scientific breakthroughs here have enabled scientists to understand much more about the human genes which may lead to incredible medical advances and financial returns. One particular area of interest is genomics, which uses industrial computing techniques to find new drugs based on the growing understanding of human genes. This could cut the costs of developing a new drug (estimated at \$800 m) by more than 30% according to the Boston Consulting Group. Not surprisingly, the share prices of many biotechnology companies have been rising even though some have yet to make a profit.

Creating a new market

Innovation can enable firms to create new markets and win business from competitors even if, at the same time, it increases costs. Take the example of

Dualit, a company that produces toasters in London and as a result has higher overheads than would be the case if it took the decision to produce in China like many of its competitors. The company recently spent £100,000, developing new heating elements that are much stronger than the usual ones found in rivals' toasters and which produce a better spread of heat. This type of technology, along with a fashionable design enables the firm to charge a premium price (over £140 for a basic toaster!). The company is committed to R&D and innovation, believing this is the way it will succeed in a market place full of competitors. In an interview with the *Sunday Times* Dualit's Managing Director said, 'Whatever pressure they may be coming under, companies need to take the long-term view. Let up on product development now and you will quickly be left behind. If everyone else is cutting back then the companies that continue to innovate will be the ones with a clear competitive advantage'.

Another highly innovative UK product was *Loaded* magazine, which was launched in the UK in 1994 by IPC magazines. According to its first editor, *Loaded* is 'for the man who believes he can do anything, if only he wasn't hung over'. At the time, it was felt there was not a mainstream market for men's magazines. *Loaded* rapidly proved this wrong, although as with all good innovations it then attracted its imitators. Imitation may be the highest form of flattery but it can also threaten a firm's existence. *FHM*, *Maxim*, and *Men's Health* all copied *Loaded*'s style, and even *GQ* started to fill its pages with semi-naked women. Commentators suspect the market is now saturated.

Leadership and innovation

The degree of innovation in business ultimately depends on its leadership – how much does it want such developments? Does it provide the necessary vision and resources? Does it reward those who innovate? Does it include innovation in its appraisals? Is communication open and cross-functional (are people talking to each other)? If you start to hear the words 'we've always done it like this', you know it's time to change something! Of course innovation also requires investment to finance the research, development and launch. In 2001 Ford produced the heaviest and most costly vehicles ever developed in the UK when it released a new Range Rover to replace the model first launched in 1970. The car costs almost £1 bn to develop. The ability to raise these kinds of funds is likely to depend on the banks' attitude to risk (unless the firm has sufficient resources itself).

The original idea

Innovation begins with ideas. These may come from various sources, such as:

- a firm's sales staff
- its laboratories
- other departments or business units in the business
- its customers.

Not that having the ideas is enough in itself. There are thousands of inventors, many of them with brilliant ideas. Trevor Baylis had the idea for a clockwork radio in 1991 and went on to develop various prototypes. He patented his invention himself but could not find anyone to help him develop the idea commercially. Fortunately his idea was eventually seen on the television programme *Tomorrow's World* and finance was provided by Christopher Staines. The product was launched in 1995 and called the Baygen Freeplay radio; 20 seconds of winding offered 40 minutes of listening.

Organisations have to try and make sure that original ideas are not passing them by. This involves:

- making sure that ideas are heard
- turning the ideas into action.

Innovation may sound simple, but in reality people worry about whether a new idea is really going to work. Managers worry about staking their career on a project that may not pay off. Banks worry about putting money into something that is unproven and investors often worry if you start talking about 'long-term' returns.

Innovation in action: JCB

In the late 1990s Anthony Bamford, the Chief Executive of JCB (the agriculture and construction equipment manufacturer), decided that the firm should diversify into the industrial handling market (forklift trucks). He created a 12-strong team to examine the figures, but at the same time stated that 'if the strategy is right we'll make the numbers work' – he was so sure that JCB could win in this market that he was prepared to do whatever was required to make it work. He even booked a place for JCB at an exhibition to launch the new product even though at that stage it was just a concept.

The idea was for a forklift truck with a telescopic arm that reached outwards rather than just lifting up and down. In a market as competitive as the forklift sector, a me-too product could not win – the only way to succeed was by developing an innovative product. Bamford's idea provided a USP (unique selling proposition) – by reaching out, it could get to places other forklifts could not, and provided better visibility for the driver. A project team was created at JCB involving suppliers, dealers and engineers. Using techniques such as critical path analysis and intensive market research of the competition, Teletruk was created on time and became a major success. Innovation helped the company to diversify successfully and was the result of senior management vision and commitment.

Patently obvious

Firms that manage to have an innovative idea may be able to patent it to provide protection against imitators. Procter and Gamble, whose brands include Pampers, Ariel and Wash and Go, has over 25,000 patents at present. A patent grants an inventor the right to stop others making the product without permission. The patent can be renewed every 12 months for up to 20 years (for a fee). To be patented an invention has to:

- be new, ie it must never have been public before (even informally)
- be inventive, ie it would not be obvious to someone who had knowledge of and experience in this area
- be capable of practical application.

At the end of its patent life, the product or process will be freely available for others to use, but even while it is in place, a patent provides information for other firms (and if they want to use it, they may be able to license it). During the 1983 America's Cup yacht race, the Australians entered the competition with a revolutionary keel. Many observers were desperate to find out more and even used deep-sea divers to try and get photos. If only they had tried the Patent Office where the patent had been published, they could have saved themselves a lot of time. Checking patents is, therefore, an important part of market research.

Summary points

- having an idea is not enough
- innovation leads to new processes and new products
- innovation can enable a firm to win customers by providing better value for money
- innovative ideas can be protected by a patent
- patents make information available to others
- the degree of innovation in an organisation depends in part on the organisation's culture and leadership

Your boss has asked you to create a proposal for next year's spending on research and development linked to turnover. What four things would you need to know to decide on a percentage of turnover that should be spent on R&D?

References

1. Philip Crosby *Quality is free: the art of making quality certain* (Signet, 1982)
2. M. Porter *Competitive Advantage* (Simon & Schuster, 1995)

The external environment of business

What is the external environment?

The success or failure of a business may lie within its control. However, it also depends on the environment in which it operates. External factors can be difficult (although not always impossible) to control; they provide an ever-changing, ever-challenging landscape in which firms compete.

The external environment can be analysed using a PEST-C framework where these letters represent:
- **P**olitical/legal factors – eg a government can affect both the demand and costs of a firm via taxation and legislation
- **E**conomic factors – eg interest rates, exchange rates and the income of the economy
- **S**ocial factors – eg pressure groups and the impact of changing social trends
- **T**echnological factors – new technology can wipe out markets or create new opportunities depending on whether a firm can exploit the changes that occur
- **C**ompetition – the degree of competition in market can affect the prices a firm charges, the pressure on organisations to innovate, the need to be efficient and the likely rate of return.

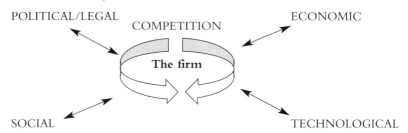

POLITICAL/LEGAL   COMPETITION   ECONOMIC

The firm

SOCIAL   TECHNOLOGICAL

Political and legal factors

The political environment can be analysed on a series of levels:
- the global environment: this involves developments that affect the world as a whole; for example, there are over 130 members of the World Trade Organisation; this organisation aims to reduce protectionism (such as tariffs and quotas) worldwide and encourage free trade
- the regional environment: this involves political change which affects particular areas of the world, eg NAFTA (the North American Free Trade Area) involves free trade between North America, Mexico and Canada

- the national environment: this involves political issues within a country, eg UK legislation affecting the running of industries such as telecommunications and water
- the local level, eg the activities of local councils.

Political action can:
- open up new markets – eg over the coming years the European Union will become significantly bigger, with ten new members joining
- bring in extra costs – eg the minimum wage was introduced in the UK in the late 1990s and increased some firm's costs
- bring additional threats – eg in 2002 the United States government decided to protect its domestic steel industry and save jobs by introducing tariffs of up to 40% on foreign imports; this hurt UK steel firms such as Corus which were used to selling a great deal of steel to America.

The legal environment can also affect business behaviour in numerous ways. It affects:
- the way staff are treated – for example, health and safety regulations, the minimum wage and employment laws

- the way firms compete – eg the government may limit the market share of a firm.

When Interbrew bought Bass for £23 bn in 2000, the Competition Commission made it sell off some of its newly acquired brands such as Carling, Caffreys and Worthington. (It was allowed to keep the Tennents, Bass Ale and Boddington's brands plus breweries in Scotland and Northern Ireland.) The Commission argued that combining the firm would form a duopoly with Scottish and Newcastle, another brewery, and have a 'common interest in raising operating margins' that would drive up net wholesale prices, increasing what consumers pay. Firms are also restricted in their ability to collude with other firms – they cannot simply set up cartels (where they fix prices and outputs) or restrict competition in markets unfairly. In 2001, for example, JCB was fined £24 m by the European Commission for a breach of competition rules; it was fined for its restrictions on sales by its distributors outside their allotted areas in the UK, France, Italy and Ireland. Restrictions had been used to stop customers buying machines at lower prices in countries other than their own. More recently, senior figures at Christie's and Sotheby's, the world famous auctioneers, were found guilty of price-fixing in a scheme that allegedly cost customers millions of dollars. Private meetings between executives of the two companies led to them fixing commission between the two auction houses rather than them competing for business.

- the way the firm markets its products – eg how it advertises and the information it provides its customers.

  A famous example of intervention in the area of marketing occurred over distribution of Wall's ice cream. In 1999 Wall's held 71% of the impulse market for ice cream with brands such as Magnum, Cornetto and Solero; this was partly achieved by offering retailers free freezers in which they had to stock Wall's products only. The Competition Commission ruled that this was anti-competitive behaviour. Most retailers did not have the space for two freezers in their stores; if they took the Wall's one, the other firms could not get access to the market. Wall's now has to make 50% of its freezer space available to rival brands.

- The government can affect a firm's success even more directly as a major purchaser of goods and services. The biggest customer of Heinz tomato ketchup is the American Army.

Government – friend or foe?

As with most things in business, whether you regard the government as a friend or foe of business depends on who you ask. 'Interventionists' believe the government is needed to control the economy and regulate business behaviour. Extreme interventionists would argue for government control of the key areas of society and the economy (eg rail, coal, gas, water, health and education) on the basis that these have a critical effect on the business environment and that they provide essential social services. Interventionists would also argue for strong regulation in areas such as employment laws (to ensure safe working conditions, reasonable pay, better consultation and to prevent discrimination) and consumer law (to prevent misleading advertising, false description of goods and unfair terms and conditions).

The other extreme is a known as a 'laissez-faire' approach. This puts more faith in the free market system. Let firms compete and the customer will benefit, they argue. Government intervention tends to be mistimed and misdirected – how can the government be expected to run areas of business properly, for example? And as for legislation, this just adds to a firm's costs, slows up decision-making and makes less people want to set up in business in the first place.

So to some the government is a saviour controlling the nasty urges of profit-seeking, non-caring business; to others it is a nuisance getting in the way of honest folk trying to do their jobs. The reality is inevitably somewhere between the two – it all depends on which aspect of government behaviour we are looking at. Some laws are probably unnecessary; others have significantly improved the way firms act towards their stakeholders. Some government-run organisations have been inefficient, but others have provided some excellent services. While services such as water and energy (and even hospitals, schools and the police) can be run by the private sector, we probably want some government regulation to ensure that we are not exploited in these essential areas.

Summary points

> • the external environment involves many different factors – political, legal, economic, social and technological

> • the political and legal environment influences a range of areas including the markets we compete in, how we market goods, how we treat employees and how we are allowed to compete

 **THINK about it!**

Think about your own organisation. Identify external factors which might affect its success. To what extent do you think its success is dependent on these external factors?

The economic environment

The economy can have a major impact on a firm's costs and demand for its products..

Economic factors

Interest rates

These affect the cost of borrowing and the reward for saving. If the interest rates increase, it is more expensive to borrow and the rewards for saving go up. This means that if a firm has borrowed money it is likely to have higher repayments, leaving less profit for other things. It also means borrowing for future projects costs more and this may deter future investment. Either way investment in new projects is likely to fall.

On the demand side, higher interest rates increases the rewards for saving. It also increases customers' repayments which may reduce their disposable income and is likely, therefore, to reduce demand. Consumers in the UK owed over £120 bn on their credit cards alone in 2001, and a large percentage of the population have borrowed on a mortgage to buy a house, so an increase in interest rates may have a fairly big effect on households!

Exchange rates

These are very important for any firm buying from or selling abroad (which must cover most UK firms these days). If the exchange rate goes up (this is known as an appreciation, a high or a strong pound) it costs more in terms of other currencies (eg $1.80 for £1 instead of $1.60). You may still be selling your goods for the same price in the UK but it now costs more for overseas buyers in their currencies to buy the pounds they need to buy your goods. To them, your goods and services seem more expensive. On the other hand, the pound under these circumstances has more purchasing power abroad and so you will find that buying goods overseas is cheaper than in pounds. A strong pound, therefore, tends to be bad for UK exporters and good for UK importers.

A big issue to do with exchange rates and the UK is whether the country enters the single European Currency (the euro) and if so at what rate. The benefits of being in the euro include lower transaction costs (because you wouldn't have to keep changing money into different currencies if you deal with other euro countries) and that it would be much easier to compare different firms' prices. On the other hand, it would involve the loss of the pound as a currency and it would mean that some aspects of economic policy such as interest rates would become more focused on Europe as a whole, not just the UK.

Gross Domestic Product (GDP)

This measures the national income in an economy. Most economies follow an economic cycle in which income goes through a boom (fast growth), recession (negative growth in the economy), slump and then recovery. The early 1980s and 1990s witnessed a recession in the UK, for example whilst the late 1980s and 1990s saw a boom.

Changes in GDP have a major effect on spending levels and therefore demand for firms' products. Some firms' products will be heavily influenced by national income (eg health clubs and champagne); others will be less dependent on income levels (eg toothpaste and socks). Changes in GDP will also influence supply conditions for a firm, eg, unemployment levels (which tend to be lower in a boom and higher in a recession) will affect the ease and cost of recruitment. The state of the economy will also affect factors such as the availability and price of land. The growth of the economy will depend on factors such as the amount of investment, spending on training, the skill and size of the workforce, the state of technology and the level of demand.

Inflation

This measures the rate at which prices in general increase in an economy. It is measured in the UK by the Retail Price Index (RPI). In the 1970s the RPI was growing at over 20% in the UK and in 2002 it was growing at around 25%.

Increasing prices affect the wage demands and expectations of staff, the competitiveness of UK firms abroad and the ease of financial planning. In times of high and unexpected inflation, many plans may have been based on false assumptions and the purchasing power of any cash or savings may be being eroded. Investment plans may need re-examining.

Inflation in an economy may be caused by excessive levels of demand pulling up prices (demand pull inflation), or increasing costs forcing firms to put up prices (cost push inflation).

Taxation

Taxes are set by the government to raise money. Direct taxes come straight from income (income tax) or profits (corporation tax); an increase in these is likely to affect consumers' ability to spend and the funds available for firms to invest. Indirect taxes such as VAT are placed on goods or services; these affect the selling price and likely sales.

Conclusion

Clearly there are enough economic factors around to keep firms on their toes. Some only change with government policy and are announced yearly in the budget, such as taxes; others, such as exchange rates, are changing all the time. Economic forecasts do exist and in some cases it is possible to predict from past trends (eg the boom, recession, recovery cycle). Even so, the economy remains something of a wild animal; sometimes tamed but never completely house-trained.

To try and control the economy the government can use:
- monetary policy: this includes setting interest rates (although in the UK, interest rates are now set by an independent body called the Monetary Policy Committee)
- fiscal policy: this uses government spending and taxation to influence supply and demand.

Given the global nature of business, it is not just the UK economy that matters to British firms. They also have to consider economies worldwide. A recession in America can affect demand from American firms and therefore UK exports. An increase in inflation in Germany can increase the costs of vital supplies from there.

Not surprisingly, some firms feel like tiny sailing boats when placed next to the huge ship of the economy – easily overrun or overturned in its wake. An increase in interest rates, for example, can increase costs and destroy your profit margins; an increase in the exchange rate can make it incredibly difficult to export. The aim of many governments is therefore to create a stable economic climate – steady growth, low predictable inflation – because this can help firms to plan.

Summary points

- there are many different factors in the economic environment: interest rate rates, exchange rates, inflation and national income

- economic factors affect the supply and demand for products

- firms can adopt strategies to protect themselves against some economic change, but it is difficult to predict all change correctly

- it is not just the UK economy that matters – the world is now interlinked to such a degree that all economies need to be observed

Choose two economic trends in the UK over the last six months. What impact might these trends have had on a) a large retailer of computer and electrical goods b) a local taxi business c) a charity organisation with its own outlets?

Social, technological and competitive factors

Social factors

Social changes include a greater awareness of environmental issues that has led to the formation and growth of pressure groups such as Greenpeace and Friends of the Earth. This has made companies examine what they produce (eg Is it environmentally friendly? Can levels of packaging be reduced?), how they produce (eg What are the emission levels and energy usage?) and where they produce (eg What is the impact on the local area?). Social issues include global warming, deforestation, exploitation of the workforce and racism.

Pressure groups exist throughout society – from the Confederation of British Industry promoting the interests of UK firms, to the Automobile Association promoting drivers' interests, to the Ramblers' Association promoting the needs of walkers. Some groups are closely consulted by the government (insider groups); others have to try and influence the government from outside (outsider groups). As society changes the key issues animating and driving pressure groups will change. The Temperance Movement (anti-alcohol) has limited support in the UK now, whereas the anti-fur movement was almost non-existent in the 1960s.

Social change also includes changes in our work and leisure patterns. Far fewer of us actually sit down for breakfast or lunch than in the past. We tend to eat on the move much more. This is known as 'snacking' or 'grazing' and has opened up market opportunities for snack products. Cadbury's launched the Fuse bar in 1996 to fill this gap in its portfolio. Faced with a decline in the breakfast cereal market, Quaker Oats joined with Swiss pharmaceuticals company, Novartis, to develop and market foods tailored to health treatment. Quaker's chief executive claimed, 'We need to change from food companies to nutrition companies'.

The increasing number of families where both partners work has also created what has become known as the 'cash rich time poor' niche that is willing to pay to have things organised for them – shirt laundries, domestic cleaning etc.

Social change opens up new opportunities for firms (eg health clubs), new challenges (eg managing a more diverse workforce) and new pressures (eg to reduce its emission levels).

It's all in the future

In a series of articles for *The Economist*, Peter Drucker, the great management writer, set out the business issues he thinks will be important in society in the future:

- There will be a rapid growth in the older population and a shrinking of the younger population in most countries. Life expectancy is generally increasing; birth rates are decreasing. This may mean that people have to keep working until their mid-70s to be able to pay for their retirement. However, they will not work in the traditional full-time, 9 am to 5pm method; they are likely to be temporary, part-timers, consultants etc. Within 20-25 years, half of the people who work for an organisation will not be employed by it. This will raise many new issues in the management of staff.

- Immigration will become a key issue. The birth rate of many developed countries is now so low that it is not sufficient to maintain stable numbers.

To keep a constant population size, several countries will need to attract younger workers from overseas. The DIW institute in Berlin estimates that Germany will have to import 1 million immigrants of working age each year simply to maintain its workforce.

- Given these changes in the age distribution we are likely to see the emergence of a middle-aged mass market and much smaller youth determined one. Products and services such as nursing homes, pension funds and private healthcare should do well.

- Due to the shortage of supply of young people, retaining staff and recruiting older people will be increasingly important for management. Tesco and B&Q in the UK have already made big efforts to recruit older staff.

- The internet provides information more rapidly – firms need to be competitive whatever business they are in because consumers can now find alternatives more easily.

- The twentieth century saw the rapid decline in the sector that had dominated society for 10,000 years: agriculture. In 1913, agriculture accounted for 70% of world trade; now its share is 17% at most. Manufacturing has travelled a long way down the same road. Since the Second World War manufacturing output has tripled in volume but prices (adjusted for inflation) have fallen steadily.

Technology

Technological change creates new products and new ways of producing, distributing and marketing products. This creates exciting but potentially threatening times. Look at almost any market you want and you can see how innovation has affected it. Tea bags have seen the introduction of round bags and then pyramid bags. Toothpaste has seen the development of gel and whitening paste. Washing powders have been challenged by the introduction of tablets and liquids. The impact of new technology on a firm will depend on whether it is riding the wave, how long the wave lasts and the reaction of other organisations.

Technology affects every aspect of business: the way we communicate, the way we work, what we produce and how we produce it. Over two million people now work from home in the UK, as tele-workers for example; because of improvements in information technology, they can still stay in contact with their businesses. There has also been a revolution in the way we design many products such as cars and aeroplanes due to Computer Aided Design (CAD). CAD has its origins in the 1950s with research done by the US Air Command; by the 1960s it was being used by companies such as General Motors. It has now been used for Evian water bottles and Cartier rings. The next major use of design software is said to be in factory design where it will be used to anticipate problems before the factory is actually built.

Competition

The degree of competition in a market will obviously influence a firm's behaviour. Greater degrees of competition are likely to lead to lower prices, more innovation and better levels of customer service. You have to offer good value for money to stay in business. On the other hand, if there is limited competition customers may suffer from poor quality and high prices because they have few alternatives. This is why governments are concerned if a few firms dominate an industry – there is the danger of collusion and of firms exploiting their customers. If one firm dominates a market, this is called a 'monopoly'. In the UK a monopoly is defined as a situation where a firm has a market share of more than 25% of a market. If several firms dominate a market it is called an 'oligopoly'. Oligopolies exist in the UK in many sectors such as food retailing, the airline industry and banking.

In 2000 and 2001 the American government was particularly worried that Microsoft was abusing its power and making it difficult for others to compete. At one point the government was insisting Microsoft would have to sell off part of its business. In the UK, regulations on competitive behaviour are enforced by the Competition Commission and follow Articles 85 and 86 of the European Union governing anti-competitive behaviour.

Summary points

- social and technological change creates new markets
- ... and destroys old ones
- organisations need to be flexible to cope with such change
- too little competition may be bad for the consumer

THINK
about it!

How do you think the education system in the UK will develop over the next ten years with developments in technology? What about the next 25 years? The next 50 years? Consider your answers to the above – if they differ, why might this be?

Competitive forces and Mr Porter

The behaviour of a firm will be affected by the conditions it faces in its markets. Michael Porter[1], professor at the Harvard Business School, developed what is now a much-used model to analyse the influences on firms, and which helps to highlight why some firms are more successful than others.

The five forces model

Porter's five forces model examines:

- the degree of competition in the market
- the supplier power
- the buyer power
- the substitute threat
- the entry threat.

Porter's 5 forces model

Degree of competition

The degree of competition will depend on factors such as:

- the growth of the market. In a declining market the sales of one firm can only be increased at the expense of another; this makes competition fairly fierce!
- the level of fixed costs. If these are high, a firm must generate high sales to cover them; this is likely to increase the degree of competition
- the exit costs (if you left, what would you lose?); if these are high, firms will fight harder to stay in the industry
- the relative size of firms in an industry; competition is likely to be higher if the industry is made up of similar sized firms rather than having a few large firms dominating

Supplier power

Supplier power considers how reliant a firm is on its suppliers of labour, money, materials and equipment. In a competitive labour market with low unemployment, for example, it may be difficult to recruit staff. This puts employees in a better bargaining position compared to employers, and may mean they can negotiate better reward packages. If there is only a limited number of suppliers and/or changing suppliers is expensive (this means high switching costs) then again the suppliers have the power at the expense of the firm. This may lead to higher costs.

Buyer power

Buyer power refers to the extent to which the customer can take his or her business elsewhere. If a buyer has lots of choices, he or she can use this to negotiate better terms.

Buyer power also depends on how important a customer is to the firm. If a firm relies on one or two key accounts, these buyers have more power than if the firm sells to millions of customers (in which case, the loss of one may not be significant).

Entry threat

This refers to the extent to which there are barriers to entry into the industry, and so influences the potential level of competition in the future. If barriers to entry are high, the entry threat is low and the pressure on existing firms is relatively low. Barriers to entry may depend on:

- whether particular licences are required to compete in a market
- the amount of investment required to start trading. Entering a market such as painting and decorating is relatively easy – it is not too expensive to start, there are lots of local markets and no major barriers to entry. By comparison, if you want to produce cars imagine the cost involved in setting up a production plant
- the existence of economies of scale. If there are large economies of scale, there is an incentive to expand to benefit from lower unit costs. This makes it difficult to compete on a small scale
- access to customers. Entry may be difficult if new firms struggle to get to the markets; for the soft drinks market, for example, it is difficult to build up a widespread distribution system quickly or cheaply. In the 1980s the Competition Commission investigated the control of pubs in the UK by the major brewers. This degree of control made it difficult for smaller brewers to find anywhere that would sell their products!

Substitute threat

This refers to the extent to which there are alternatives to the firm's products. This may be a direct substitute (such as switching from one brand of cigarettes to another) or simply other products that compete for the same spending (eg you may be choosing between another holiday abroad or a new sofa).

Conclusion

Firms operating in sectors where supplier power is weak, buyer power is weak, the entry threat, substitute threat and degree of rivalry are low are likely to be more successful than those operating where the conditions are the opposite.

According to Porter, firms should seek to answer the following questions when developing their strategy:

■ How can they reduce the bargaining power of their customers and suppliers? Can they find alternative suppliers, for example, or develop another customer base?

■ How can they reduce the existence of perceived substitutes to their products? Can they develop a unique selling point, for example?

■ How can they reduce the amount of competition in its market? Can they takeover rivals, for example?

■ How can they make it more difficult for other firms to enter the market?

Summary points

▶ Porter's five forces model can be used to analyse market conditions

▶ firms can try to shape conditions in their favour

▶ the five forces change over time, affecting the nature of the market

Think about the UK food retail sector. Using Porter's five forces model, decide on the most important factors under each heading.

Opportunities and threats

The external environment creates opportunities and threats for firms. Organisations need to consider their opportunities and relate them back to their strengths and weaknesses (this is called SWOT analysis). Relevant opportunities should be exploited. At the same time, organisations must protect themselves against threats.

Opportunities

- New laws may create new markets, eg, regulations affecting emissions may create the opportunity for firms to develop products and processes which meet these new requirements.
- Lower interest rates may reduce the cost of borrowing, enabling more investment.
- Social change may create new markets, such as the rising demand for healthier food and environmentally friendly products.
- Technological factors may provide the opportunity for a firm to produce and benefit from new products. The computer games market is relatively young and yet has overtaken films in terms of market size.

Threats

- A high exchange rate may make exporting difficult for a UK firm (because it makes UK goods more expensive in terms of foreign currency).
- Pressure groups may prevent a firm going ahead with a project. For example, when BAA proposed a new Terminal 5 at Heathrow, it took eight years, £80 m and 80,000 documents to receive permission from the government, against fierce resistance from protesters worried about the impact on the local community and wildlife.
- Technological development makes products obsolete – how many typewriters are sold in the UK now? how much longer will video cassettes continue to sell against DVDs?
- The government may pass legislation which increases costs, eg more stringent healthy and safety laws.

The effect of external change on an organisation depends on the precise nature of the change and the internal position of the firm – is it in a position to exploit the changes created? What may be a threat for one firm could be an opportunity for another. Take the downturn in the world economy and the after-shock of the September 11th hijackings in 2001. For many airlines, this led to a drop in demand; in some cases it accelerated their decline and even led to closure. Swissair went bankrupt, while many other airlines such as British Airways (BA) and American Airlines made major redundancies. However, not all airlines suffered. Some were able to benefit from this situation. RyanAir and EasyJet, for example, both enjoyed increased sales and profits. Why? Because given lower incomes in the economy, people switched to lower price journeys. While BA's passenger numbers fell by 11.5% on the year before, in November 2001 EasyJet's rose by 38.5%. On the supply side, the smaller airlines also benefited from the closure of the larger ones – they were able to get pilots more easily and planes more cheaply. In 2001 EasyJet and Ryanair announced major expansion plans.

Summary points

▶ external forces can create opportunities and threats – it depends on how a firm reacts to change

▶ the relative importance of different factors in the external environment will differ from firm to firm

THINK about it!

You are a car manufacturer. Identify three possible opportunities and threats facing the industry in the next ten years.

Social responsibility

Organisations are continually interacting with a wide range of groups and individuals. These include their employees, investors, suppliers, customers, the communities they operate in, pressure groups and the government. Firms produce goods and services that we then consume. They are also responsible for much of our lives as employees. They also produce waste products and affect the quality of life in the areas in which they operate. They create wealth. They move society forward with innovations or hold it back by restricting competition. Their managers set an example (good or bad) by their behaviour.

Given this degree of interaction with the world around them, firms must decide on the extent to which they accept their social responsibilities. Social responsibility is the obligation of managers to choose and act in ways that benefit both the interests of the organisation and those of society as a whole. Decisions by organisations inevitably impact on other groups, and managers must consider whether or not to take these effects into account.

Take the decision by the government to let a national lottery be run in the UK. This involved numerous social issues – would it encourage gambling? Would it take money away from charities? Would it act as a form of tax on lower income groups who were the most likely to take part? Similarly, a decision by Sainsbury's supermarket to open a large out-of-town store raises many questions concerning social responsibility: the new store may take away business from town centre shops and force them to close. This may create unemployment and contribute to the decline of that area. Is this acceptable? There may also be people who are unable to get to the new out-of-town stores – should we care about them? And what about the impact on the area where the superstore is built in terms of house prices, traffic, noise and litter? A key issue facing firms therefore is the extent to which the views and needs of different groups in society are considered in decision making.

Opinions on social responsibility

Views about a firm's social obligations vary significantly. According to Milton Friedman, the idea of business being socially responsible is fundamentally flawed. To Friedman, 'The business of business is business … there is only one social responsibility of business – to use its resources and engage in activities designed to increase its profits so long as it stays within the rules of the game, engages in open and free competition, without deception and fraud'. Compare this with the views of Tomorrow's Company, an organisation set up to promote the concept of social responsibility in business. Tomorrow's Company proposes that a successful organisation 'values reciprocal relationships, understanding that by focusing on and learning from all those who contribute to the business it will be able to improve returns to shareholders … works actively to build reciprocal relationships with customers, suppliers, and other key stakeholders through a partnership approach.'

There are numerous arguments in favour of acting socially responsibly (although each social issue may need to be considered on its own merits). For example:

- it can attract (or retain) staff because some employees will want to be associated with a socially responsible employer
- it can use its behaviour in its marketing. The Cooperative Bank in the UK has successfully positioned itself as the ethical bank since 1992. It portrays itself as a bank that listens to its customers and behaves in a socially responsible manner. It has found a niche that enables it to compete against

the large banks, such as Barclays and HSBC, and attract 2.5 m customers. In pursuing socially responsible values, the Cooperative Bank has managed to tap into a segment of the market that wanted a bank which would think more carefully about who it lent it to and how it behaved
- it can encourage investors and boost the share price
- it can ensure the firm is ready should the law change to make certain behaviours compulsory
- it can avoid adverse publicity.

Firms attacked for their behaviour: Nike and Barclays Bank

In the 1990s Nike faced much criticism for the way staff were treated in some of its overseas manufacturing plants. This led to student protests and boycotting of its products. In May 1998, chief executive Phillip Knight admitted that 'Nike has become synonymous with slave wages, forced overtime and arbitrary abuse'. Nike has had to work very hard to change these perceptions and win back favour with its customers, by convincing them it now acts in a socially responsible manner. Interestingly, Nike has been held responsible for conditions in the factories where its products have been made, even though it does not actually own them. The concept of social responsibility is so broad nowadays that firms are often held accountable for their suppliers.

In 2000 Barclays Bank was heavily criticised when it decided to axe 172 of its branches, leaving many communities across the country without High Street banking facilities. This was part of a £1 bn cost-cutting programme. Leading UK charities representing the elderly, pressure groups representing small businesses and the Campaign for Community Banking Services all fought against this move by the bank. In its defence, Barclays said that the closures were the result of fewer customers using counter services, poor sales of financial products in the 172 branches and poor prospects. It added that if Barclays had to keep open a bank in each of the UK's 25,000 towns and villages it would be bankrupt tomorrow.

Summary points

- social responsibility is the extent to which a firm accepts it obligations to its stakeholder groups over and above its legal requirements

- some commentators, such as Friedman, think the concept of social responsibility is a distraction; others believe that acting socially responsibly is important

Should a firm be held responsible for the actions of its suppliers?

Stakeholders and firms' behaviour

Social responsibility involves a firm's obligations to its stakeholder groups. A stakeholder is an individual or group inside or outside the organisation who affects or is affected by its activities. Even if we accept that a firm should have some responsibility to groups such as its employees, its suppliers and the local community, some fairly fundamental questions still remain – exactly whose interests should be served and how far should organisations go in meeting the needs of specific stakeholder groups? Is one group of stakeholders more important than another?

Medelow's model

To help firms decide which stakeholder groups might be of most importance, managers may undertake stakeholder mapping using Medelow's model. This compares a stakeholder group's power with its interest in the firm's strategy.

		LEVEL OF INTEREST	
		Low	High
POWER	Low	A	B
	High	C	D

- Group A has limited power and limited interest in the firm, and so minimal effort is likely to be made to keep this group happy.
- Group B is interested in the firm's activities but has limited power. Firms are likely to try and keep these groups informed but will probably do little more than this.
- Group C has a low level of interest at the moment but is powerful and may become more interested over time or in reaction to a specific event (eg oil spillage). Firms will usually try to keep these groups satisfied.
- Group D is the group of 'key players' – managers will probably want to make sure they agree with a strategy before going ahead. This is because they are not only interested in the organisation but are also powerful. Their power may lie in the number of members they have, or their access to the media or the government.

While the precise nature of a firm's reaction to a stakeholder group will depend on the issue and the features of that group, as seen above, general modes of behaviour of firms can be categorised as:

- **obstructive** – this occurs when an organisation denies responsibility and resists change
- **defensive** – this occurs when a firm gradually moves towards a more socially responsible stance but only as and when it is pushed. Such firms will try to resist and justify their original actions. They will try to stick to the legal minimum requirements
- **adaptive** – in this approach a company accepts it is accountable for its actions and adapts to the requirements of a situation, but does not seek to lead the way
- **proactive** – this occurs when a company takes the lead in social issues. It regards business as an important force within society and sees itself as a positive force for change.

Increasing social responsibility: Shell

A company that has become noticeably more socially responsible in recent years is the multinational oil company, Shell plc. The company faced very negative public opinion following the execution of human rights campaigner and author Ken Saro Wiwa and eight others in Nigeria. Shell was criticised for the environmental damage it allegedly caused in the country and for not supporting human rights campaigners such as Saro Wiwa.

Shell fought back, stating that its investment in Nigeria created jobs, but it is generally agreed it lost the media war. Shell was also heavily attacked in the media by the pressure group Greenpeace for the way it intended to dispose of the Brent Spar oil rig in the North Sea in 1996. Facing very high levels of scrutiny and criticism from numerous groups, Shell has now moved towards a much more open position in the last few years.

Shell's website (www.shell.com) states: 'The objectives of the Royal Dutch/Shell Group of companies are to engage efficiently, responsibly and profitability in the oil, gas, chemicals, and other selected businesses and participate in the research and development of other sources of energy. We must deliver and be seen to deliver in two ways. We need the profitability that provides the competitive returns and funds investment ... Shell companies also accept their responsibility to help deliver the economic, social and environmental requirements of sustainable development. Being trusted to meet societal expectations is essential for long-term profitability. We are committed to transparency and to developing and integrating our reporting'.

Notice that the company does not believe that social responsibility and profits are mutually exclusive. It believes one enhances the other.

Balancing act

There are numerous stakeholder groups, all of which have an interest in a business. Managers must decide which groups they acknowledge and the extent to which they will attempt to meet the needs and wishes of such groups. Given the firm's limited resources and the numerous demands on it from various stakeholder groups, managers may well be performing something of a balancing act. Managers may have to decide which issues or groups to focus on and, at times, make difficult decisions about priorities. Barclays defended its decision to close local bank branches on the basis that if it didn't it would fail to make a profit.

Summary points

- ▶ stakeholders are groups or individuals which are affected by a firm's activities
- ▶ organisations have to consider how to react to the different demands of the various stakeholder groups; each group is likely to have its own demands and objectives
- ▶ the reaction of firms may vary from being obstructive to being proactive

THINK
about it!

Think about the organisation where you work or study. Identify three key stakeholder groups. What factors determine the power of these groups? Can you think of examples where they have changed the organisation's behaviour?

Social responsibility in action

The Body Shop

The Body Shop is one of the best-known socially responsible companies in the UK, if not the world. As it says on the company website: 'The Body Shop has always believed that business is primarily about human relationships. We believe that the more we listen to our stakeholders and involve them in decision making, the better our business will run. In 1999 The Body Shop was voted the second most trusted brand in the UK by the Consumers Association ... The Body Shop is a stakeholder-led company. It believes its success is dependent upon its relationships with all its stakeholders, including employees, franchisees, customers, communities, suppliers, shareholders and Non-Government Organisations (NGOs).'

The company was founded by entrepreneur Anita Roddick in 1976, when she started retailing homemade and naturally inspired products using minimal packaging. The business rapidly grew from one small shop in Brighton, on the South coast of England, with only around 25 hand-mixed products on sale to a worldwide network of shops. The Body Shop campaigns against human rights abuses and in favour of animal and environmental protection, and is committed to challenging the stereotypes of beauty perpetuated by the cosmetics industry. It has turned a niche of environmentally safe products into a mass market and its success has led to numerous imitators worldwide.

In 1995 the company put its beliefs to the test when it agreed to its first social audit alongside its existing audits of its environmental activities. The results of these activities are independently verified and published in The Values Report. The Body Shop is a good example of a business that has benefited from acting in a socially responsible manner. Customers have identified with its values and this has created a major marketing advantage for the business. When you buy from The Body Shop, you are buying into the company's strong beliefs about how business should behave; many people are clearly willing to pay for this.

Ben and Jerry's

Another famous and successful values-led business is Ben and Jerry's, which is based in Vermont, USA. The ice cream-making company aims to maximise its social impact by integrating socially beneficial actions into as many of its day-to-day activities as possible. For example, if the firm is considering three different options for a new flavour, the founders state that 'being values-led means choosing the one that gives the best opportunity to integrate our commitment to social change with the need to return reasonable profits to our shareholders. Assuming all three flavours are profitable, if we find out that we can make one of them using nuts from the rainforest (in order to increase economic demand for the living rain forest) and we can put the ice cream in a rainforest themed container that raises awareness about the problem of rainforest deforestation, we would choose that flavour'. This is exactly what they did with the Rainforest Crunch flavour. This approach to decision-making has given Ben and Jerry's ice cream a very clear 'alternative' identity, which distinguishes it from other ice cream makers. You are not just buying excellent ice cream when you buy Ben and Jerry's, you are buying an attitude.

In their book *Double Dip*, Ben and Jerry state that there are five key points to remember in business:

- business is the most powerful force in society. Therefore, business has a responsibility for the welfare of society as a whole
- a values-led business can be highly profitable
- people can influence business – as investors, employees, consumers
- Ben and Jerry are two regular guys who succeeded in a large part because they were true to themselves
- there's a spiritual aspect to business.

Summary points

▶ The Body Shop has led the way on social responsibility for nearly 30 years

▶ Ben and Jerry have shown values-led business can work and be profitable, however they stress that it's not easy. There are always new challenges and new issues to deal with

Is it worth being socially responsible?

Business and ethics

There has been an increasing interest in the role of ethics in business in recent years. Ethics involve decisions about what is right and wrong. An ethical issue is one where there is a choice between alternatives and these alternatives will affect others. There are, of course, laws that govern individuals' and firms' behaviour, but the legal framework does not cover all situations. It is these uncertain areas where a decision about ethics is most significant. Our ethics depend on what we value, what we believe is fair, what rights we think we and others have.

Businesspeople naturally face all kinds of dilemmas where they must make a choice about what is the right thing to do. Imagine you have developed a new cure for Aids or cancer; there is obviously a huge demand for such a product, so should you charge as much for it as you can, or offer a lower price so that more people can benefit from using it? What if you have the opportunity to expand your production but the building and additional production may have an impact on the environment, the local community and wildlife in the area? Or what if you are worried about your company's share price – do you encourage your finance team to window dress your accounts to flatter the figures?

The growth in the interest in business ethics was partly due to the unacceptable behaviour of companies in the 1960s and 1970s. One company in particular that was criticised in America for its activities was International Telephone and Telegraph (ITT). Under the leadership of Harold Geneen in the 1970s managers at ITT – a huge conglomerate – seemed to believe they could get away with almost anything provided it was profitable. 'For Harold Geneen the only line was the bottom line (ie profit)' said his obituary in *The Times*. ITT employed bribery and coercion as part of its general business tactics; it funded illegal operations around the world and worked with the American Central Intelligence Agency to overthrow President Allende's left-wing government in Chile where ITT had a substantial business. The revulsion at ITT's activities helped produce a backlash that led to demands for higher standards of business morality.

What is 'right' and 'wrong'?

Deciding what is and what is not ethical is no easy matter. After all, your view of what is right and wrong may differ from mine. When considering the ethics of a situation, should a manager think about it from his or her personal perspective, or those of the owners (these perspectives may conflict)? And on what basis should the decision be made: should managers only take actions that they personally agree with? Or should they use some rule of thumb such as avoiding any action that would tend to make more people worse off than it makes better off? Should they try and act in the interests of the majority? But what if the majority is wrong?

Almost inevitably some groups will win and others will lose as the result of any decision – how do we decide which are most important groups? How do we value the needs of different groups? What if we stop producing one of our products that is proved to be harmful to the environment? The environment may be better off, but what about our employees who may lose their jobs? Or our suppliers who lose business? Or our investors who lose their rewards? How can we assess and value the impact on these different groups?

Of course, managers do not work in a vacuum and it is not just a question of what they personally want to do. In many ways managers are in a goldfish bowl examined by the media and numerous pressure groups. The decision about what is and what is not ethical may therefore be out of their hands. Take the cocoa industry – outrage at the use of child labour in African countries such as the Ivory Coast prompted an international protocol agreement governing the industry, which commits global chocolate makers to eliminating child labour within the next ten years.

Knowing the 'right' thing to do can sometimes be very difficult. In 2001, for example, Andrew Millar suspected that the press releases of the company he worked for (British Biotech) were misleading, suggesting that the firm's progress developing a cure for cancer was more advanced than it actually was. To find out the truth Millar had to access confidential files. Millar's boss accused Millar of acting unethically by getting hold of the files and fired him. Others criticised him for releasing confidential data to the press and 'blowing the whistle' on his company. Millar, meanwhile, accused the company of being unethical for misleading investors. He was later compensated by the company for the loss of his job.

Another ethical issue that created a major storm in the UK in the mid-1990s was the launch of alcoholic soft drinks. The sector was created by such brands as Hooper's Hootch (Bass), Lemonheads (Carlsberg Tetley), and Two Dogs (Merrydown) and provided a valuable boost to the brewers. The drinks industry was attacked by consumer pressure groups who claimed that the packaging and marketing of these drinks was appealingly too strongly to underage drinkers. Under attack by the media, manufacturers moved quickly to rebrand and repackage. Companies such as Whitbread changed the proposed names of new products to make them more adult and the drinks were then sold in bottles, not cans. At its peak in 1996 Hooper's Hootch sold 370,000 barrels. Hostile public opinion and restrictions of marketing activities meant this fell to under 150,000 by the end of 1998.

Dealing with ethics

How does an organisation deal with ethical issues? One approach is to create a whole series of rules and regulations that attempt to cover every conceivable situation. The problem with this is that it is difficult to regulate for every eventuality. Leave a gap and someone will sneak through it. Alternatively, an organisation might try and demonstrate to employees what the senior managers believe are the key values they must hold, and leave them free to apply these as they see fit. Many organisations now have a Code of Conduct setting out general principles that they expect their employees to follow. Nike produced its Code in 1992, for example. Whether these are adhered to depends on the culture within the firm and whether rewards are linked to behaviour that fits with the Code. Levi Strauss, for example, builds into its appraisals an assessment of whether someone has managed according to its code.

Ethics don't stand still

It is important to remember that our views of what is and what is not acceptable can and will change over time. As the years go by our standards change and we seem to expect ever more information to be provided by organisations about their activities and ever-higher standards of behaviour. In 2002, an increase in the number of street crimes where mobile phones were stolen led to demands that the mobile phone companies make their products more difficult for thieves to use. They were almost blamed for the crimes!

Summary points

- ethical issues arise whenever decisions have to be made
- ethics concern what is right and wrong
- what is and is not ethical is not always easy to decide; what you think is acceptable I may not, and vice versa
- there has been more scrutiny of firms' ethics in the media in recent years
- pressure groups can force firms to change their behaviour

- A customer wants to buy a blue dress. You know she looks better in the red one and that the blue one does not fit her properly. Do you let her buy the blue dress? What is the reason for your decision?
- You are an estate agent trying to sell a property on behalf of your clients. You know there is damp in the walls of the property but the potential buyers do not ask about it. Do you tell them? What is your reasoning?
- You have built up a business locally for the last ten years. The local community has been very cooperative and you are a major employer. The savings of moving production to the Far East are significant and you are considering moving. Identify three key factors which would help you to decide whether or not to relocate.
- Your advertising agency has been approached by a company to advertise its products. These are manufactured overseas and there have been many allegations about the way in which they are produced, such as child labour and poor working conditions. Identify two key pieces of information you would like to have before deciding whether to accept the contract or not.

Globalisation

A significant trend in the last few decades has been the increasing trade between countries and the extent to which firms are now operating internationally. We are truly living and consuming in a global economy. Just look at companies such as General Motors, Ford, Shell, Exxon, Toyota and IBM which produce and sell all over the world. In the words of Hill[2], 'Globalisation refers to the shift towards a more integrated and interdependent world economy. Globalisation has two main components: the globalisation of markets and the globalisation of production'. More products are being sold worldwide; more firms are sourcing their suppliers globally. Inevitably this process of globalisation presents both challenges and opportunities for organisations.

Why is globalisation happening?

- **Technology** – Theodore Levitt[3] argues that technology is the real driving force behind globalisation: 'A powerful force drives the world toward a converging commonality and that force is technology. It has proletarianised communication, transport and travel. It has made isolated places and impoverished peoples eager for modernity's allurements. Almost everyone everywhere wants all the things they have heard about, seen or experienced via the new technologies. The result is a new commercial reality – the emergence of global markets for standardised consumer products on a previously unimagined scale of magnitude.' According to Levitt, global companies will benefit so much from large-scale production that no one else will be able to compete. However, while it is true that globalisation has occurred in some markets (cars and electronics, for example), it is far from common in all sectors.
- **Cost advantages** – economies of scale are naturally tempting and attractive. By going global, firms may be able to build enough demand to justify large-scale production and enjoy lower unit costs. These economies of scale may be concerned with production or marketing. Promoting a brand worldwide, for example, enables you to spread the costs.
- **The growth of global brands** – almost wherever you go in the world people are wearing Levis, eating a McDonald's, drinking a Coca Cola and smoking a Marlboro. There is, it seems, less and less to divide us when it comes to goods and services.
- **Fewer barriers to exports and imports** – within the European Union (EU), for example, there has been a greater harmonisation of standards making it easier for UK firms to sell in member countries.
- **Operating in several countries** also allows firms to exploit the favourable conditions of each one, eg it may want to benefit from cheaper materials, cheaper labour or less stringent safety requirements.

Global firms: Gillette, Tesco

One company that clearly pursues the global approach is Gillette, the US razor maker; over 60% of its sales are outside its home base of the US. To Gillette the world is made up of lots of people needing a shave! It refuses to pay any attention to cultural differences. 'A multinational has operations in different countries. A global company views the world as a single country. We know Argentina and France are different but we treat them the same. We sell them the same products, we use the same production methods, we have the same corporate policies. We even use the same advertising, in a different language of course,' said its Chief Executive. Its one-size-fits-all marketing strategy has been extremely effective: its share of the worldwide shaving market is 70%.

However, it may not be so easy for other products to be marketed in the same way because of greater national and cultural differences. Tesco, for example, sees the appeal of reacting to local markets. In its Korean store in Seoul you can buy a pet iguana or an octopus, visit the dentist or even take ballet lessons. Rather than just rushing into the new market, Tesco entered into an alliance with Samsung (with the latter taking a 19% stake in the venture); this helped ensure that Tesco understood the market and was accepted by the local business community.

How to go global

There are often various stages a firm will go through before becoming truly global. Typically these include:
- exporting from a home base, eg a UK firm starts to sell overseas
- if exports are relatively high a firm may consider setting up a base overseas; at this stage each base tends to operate independently
- if the overseas markets continue to be of interest, the third stage is often becoming a multinational operating and planning in several countries. At this stage the top managers may be drawn from all over the organisation but the business tends to dominated by its home headquarters. In a multinational approach the home country and home managers tend to be at the centre of most decision making
- the final stage of development occurs when an organisation becomes truly transnational. This means that the company has businesses all over the world and all of these have a similar status. They operate as a network of equals in which each country is represented fully at a senior level. No one country (such as the home country of the firm) dominates.

The downside to going global

The danger of going global is that you treat the world as if it is the same, when in fact underlying differences remain. The result is that you may end up with a standardised product that fails to satisfy because it does not quite hit the spot.

The alternative is to go local and produce different items for different markets. The trouble with this is it may be expensive to produce many different versions of your product. A compromise is to 'think global and act local'. This attempts to standardise wherever possible, but still build in differences for local markets. For example, Whirlpool, which makes white goods such a fridges and freezers, produces fairly standard component parts. However, these are combined in different ways to meet the needs of different markets with particular features added for different markets.

Global firms – bad boys?

Some of the multinational firms that now exist are huge and have enormous influence. Several pressure groups believe such firms often abuse their power, eg by exploiting labour and pressurising governments to prevent some types of legislation going through. Anti-globalisation protests (such as the major rally in Seattle in 1999) now hit the news fairly regularly as campaigners try to ensure that multinationals and governments act socially responsibly and do not abuse their power.

Globalisation problems: B&Q

The DIY retailer B&Q has experienced difficulties operating abroad. B&Q was one of the first British retailers to enter mainland China. However, it discovered many significant differences with the UK such as:
- homeowners in China have few incentives to undertake DIY because there is a big labour pool of migrant labour that will do the work
- holidays in China are limited and few people have a spare room or garage to serve as a workshop for DIY
- the housing market is radically different – new houses in China usually have nothing in them and to fix them up is not really a DIY job; there are often no floors, no plaster on the walls, no kitchen or bathroom units. Typical customers are young couples about to marry or who have just bought a flat; they are often accompanied by the person who will carry out the decoration as work. The couple decide on colours and styles whilst the workman grills sales staff with detailed technical questions.

Summary points

- globalisation has many attractions such as access to more markets and the possibility of gaining economies of scale ...

- however, the world remains full of different markets. This makes globalisation less easy for some products than others

- even if you do go global the need to think local remains; customers still act and think differently in different parts of the world

Think about the times you have been abroad or when you have seen foreign countries on television. Identify three brands of goods and three brands of services that you would expect to find in most countries. Why do think these brands have been successful? Do you think it is easier to be global with some kinds of products and services than others? Why? Do you think it has become easier or more difficult for products to succeed globally? Why?

References

1. M. Porter *Competitive Advantage* (Simon & Schuster, 1995).
2. C. Hill *International Business* (McGraw Hill, 2000).
3. Theodore Levitt 'The Globalisation of Markets' *Harvard Business Review* Vol 61.3 (1983)

Change, the future and success

Change

The management of change is very important. As most business books say, 'change is the one constant in business'. Just look at the music industry: Mariah Carey was the biggest selling female artist of the 1990s, selling 120 m records worldwide. In 2002 she was paid nearly £20 m by EMI *not* to sing for them anymore!

Change may be internal (employees wanting to leave their jobs) or external (a change in the economic climate). It may be slow (the increasing interest in environmental issues) or fast (a sudden increase in the exchange rate). Even if you do not want to change, your competitors almost certainly will, and so just to stand still you need to be able to match what they do.

The riskiest thing of all in business is to do nothing. At least if you bring about change you may or may not get it right; if you do nothing you will almost certainly get it wrong. Whatever worked for you in the past is unlikely to be working for you in the future. The dangers of resisting change are neatly highlighted by the business writer Charles Handy[1]: 'If you put a frog in cold water and slowly heat it, the frog will eventually let itself be boiled to death. We, too, will not survive if we don't respond to the radical way in which the world is changing.' We are all vulnerable to change, even the PG Tips chimps. After 45 years of appearing in television adverts the chimps were replaced in 2002 by animated birds produced by Aardvark Animations, the Oscar winning company that produced Wallace and Grommit. 2002 also saw the end of Cats the musical after 21 years of success in the West End.

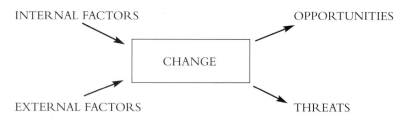

Change creates both opportunities and threats. The rise of mobile phones enabled Vodafone to grow at a tremendous rate – it acquired over 100 m customers in a matter of years. But no firm can sit back and relax: Netscape Navigator invented the web browser (the software that allows you to access the internet); now it is but a minor player next to Microsoft's Internet Explorer which has 80% of the market. In 2002 Vodafone announced the largest loss in UK corporate history at that time.

The following quotes make clear the importance of understanding the process and management of change:

- 'The nineties will be a decade in a hurry, a nanosecond culture. There'll be only two kinds of managers – the quick and the dead'. *David Vice, Chief Executive of Northern Telecom*
- 'Every organisation has to prepare for the abandonment of everything it does'. *Peter Drucker, Harvard Business Review*
- 'Change. Change. Change. We must learn to deal with it, thrive on it. That's todays' relentless refrain. But it's incorrect. Astoundingly we must move beyond change and embrace nothing less than the literal abandonment of the conventions that brought us to this point. Eradicate "change" from your vocabulary. Substitute "abandonment" or "revolution" instead'. *Tom Peters, 'The Tom Peters Seminar – crazy times call for crazy organisations'*

Methods of producing change

Lewin's three-stage model

To help analyse the process of bringing about change, Kurt Lewin[2] proposed a three-stage model:

This involves:

- **unfreezing**: individuals will have set values and ways of doing things. The first stage in a change process is to make them lose these values. This can be done by making the need for change so obvious that individuals and teams understand why it must happen and accept it. According to Bob Lutz, former Vice Chairman of Chrysler, change is 'just a question of getting people to accept that it's okay to step out of their comfort zone, which is the way they've always done it and to be willing to take a risk on trying something new'
- **leadership**: once employees are open to a new way of doing things, managers must promote new values and attitudes. As Sir Peter Bonfield, Chief Executive at BT says, 'you cannot achieve change unless you have everybody, in their minds and their hearts, believing that they're a part of it, that they think it's the right thing to do, and they will put up with the inconveniences that change always produce'
- the final stage is known as '**refreezing**'; this involves locking the new methods and values into place by supporting and reinforcing mechanisms, eg it may involve rewarding the new behaviour and punishing, or at least not rewarding, the old.

| UNFREEZE | → | LEADERSHIP | → | REFREEZE |

Kotter and Schlesinger: managing change

In their famous study, Kotter and Schlesinger[3] identified several ways in which change might be brought about:

- communication – people will usually want to know: Why are we doing this? What do we need to know? Who will be in charge of what? Managers leading change need to ensure that these questions are answered at the start of the process of change
- facilitation and support – this involves reassuring people, showing them that it will work and giving them the time, training and resources they need to adjust properly
- participation – people are more likely to commit to something if they feel they own the decision, so it may be worth involving them in the process
- negotiation – it may be a question of give and take and compromise
- manipulation and co-option – if necessary, you may need to be cunning. For example, you might remove the ringleader of the resistance to the change or try to win him or her over first with rewards; once the ringleader is on board, others will follow
- coercion – if all else fails, you may have to push change through regardless and force others to accept.

Kaizen – little change daily

This is a Japanese approach to change which stands for continuous improvement. It believes that business performance can increase significantly through ongoing incremental change – it does not need sudden and dramatic shifts. Under a kaizen approach, employees are encouraged to contribute and suggest ways of improving the way jobs are done. Gradual improvement builds over time to major progress. It is a system that builds on employees' experiences and skills and requires good two-way communication.

Reengineering – big change less regularly

Whilst kaizen has an appeal, some commentators think it is too half-hearted. Kaizen may improve the way you do what you are doing at the moment, but what if what you are doing is wrong to begin with? It may be that a much more fundamental change is needed to have real impact.

In the 1990s a management approach called reengineering became popular. This was pioneered by James Champy and Michael Hammer[4]. Unlike kaizen supporters, Champy and Hammer want firms to contemplate a complete overhaul of everything they do. Reengineering demands that organisations throw away any preconceived ideas about the way they do things and be prepared to start planning again on a blank piece of paper. 'Business reengineering isn't about fixing anything. Business reengineering means starting all over, starting from scratch' claim Champy and Hammer in their book, *Reengineering the Corporation*. Hammer's advice is 'don't automate, obliterate'. It may be better to do without operations than make them more efficient.

While the idea of organisations examining their very essence has value, reengineering has become associated with large-scale redundancies. Some managers have used the concept as a way of introducing unpleasant changes within the firm; by calling it 'reengineering', this somehow gives it a form of legitimacy. There is no doubt some firms such as Lloyds Bank have benefited from reengineering and have made important changes to the way they operate by being prepared to stand back and rip out; others however have seen it simply as an excuse to sack people – there has been no fundamental change apart from redundancy.

Summary points

- change is the one constant in the business environment
- change may be internal or external
- managing change is a key element of the management process
- people are likely to resist change so be prepared for this
- there are various ways of overcoming resistance to change, from simply explaining why it is necessary to forcing it through
- some change is incremental such as kaizen; progress occurs gradually
- some change is radical such as reengineering; progress occurs very suddenly

THINK about it!

Think about a situation at your work or college where change was introduced and resisted. Why was it resisted? Could this resistance have been overcome? Do you think the process of change was handled well or badly? Why?

Looking to the future

Managers must look ahead to predict where the business is heading. For example, they need some idea of the likely level of sales because this will then affect cash-flow forecasts, their human resource plans and their production scheduling. These forecasts may be based on past data. You may try and identify the underlying trend in the past and then project it forwards – this is known as extrapolation. Or you may rely on experts to help you form an opinion of where your sales are heading. These may be industry experts or experts within your own business. If the market is changing rapidly or you don't have much backdata then using expert opinion to form a view is most likely to be useful to you.

Forecasting – the pitfalls

Forecasting is inevitably dangerous because so many things can change and developments in markets can be difficult to predict. Nearly 60 years ago, IBM chairman Thomas Watson said 'I think there is a world market for maybe five computers'. Nearly one billion personal computers have been sold in the past 20 years, compared with 300 million cars.

Forecasting is especially difficult if markets are new or changing rapidly, such as the internet; telecoms companies invested so heavily in licences for 3G (third generation) technology, only to find they were far too optimistic about when it would actually arrive in the market place. A huge number of dot.com companies over-predicted their sales and collapsed in the late 1990s.

Bill Gates, billionaire boss of Microsoft, reckoned that 50% of groceries would be ordered online by 2005. The more restrained Institute of Grocery Distributors predicted a shift of between 23–27% by 2008. The actual figure is likely to be closer to 1%, and many leading players in this market have suffered as a result of the slower than expected take up. Asda and Sainsbury remain very quiet about their success in e-commerce, while Iceland, which actually started rebranding its stores as Iceland.co.uk stopped this policy presumably because of revised forecasts of its e-commerce sales. The one clear winner so far in UK internet retailing is Tesco, delivering over 70,000 orders per week (although, to put this in perspective, it serves 12 m customers per week). Interestingly, Tesco succeeded by using the simplest model – it did not build separate picking centres to keep the food (unlike Asda and Sainsbury); it used its own stores.

Some firms also use scenario planning. This technique was pioneered by the Royal Dutch Shell Company. It uses experts to picture several alternative situations in the future. Its aim is to predict general large-scale movements in markets rather than specifically trying to identify an exact sales level. The Shell planners examine the data which their planning department and other experts have collected, and form possible versions of what the future might hold. Aris de Geus, Shell's former head of planning, says in his book, *The Living Company* that scenario planning helped the company foresee the energy crises of 1973 and 1979, the growth of energy conservation and the break up of the Soviet Union. The strength of the approach was evident in early 1980s when the price of a barrel of oil was hovering around $30. With exploration and development costs averaging at $11 a barrel most oil companies were making record profits and feeling very confident. Shell created various scenarios, one of which was the breakdown of OPEC cartel that restricted the world supply of oil; the predicted result was a glut and a drop in oil prices to $15 per barrel. By 1986 the consequences of the 'game' included efforts to cut exploration costs by pioneering advanced exploration technologies, massive investments and weeding out the least profitable service stations. By April 1986 price of oil fell to $10 per barrel. Shell had a head-start because, unlike the others, it had already begun considering cost-cutting techniques.

However, some analysts, such as Mintzberg, criticise scenario planning on the basis that the chances of a particular scenario coming to pass are slim. 'The idea of sitting down and saying "what are the possibilities?" is fine, but who would have predicted what happened in New York [*on September 11th*]?'.

Summary points

▶ planning is important to firms

▶ planning is difficult

▶ sometimes you might use the past; sometimes you might ask the experts

▶ other times you might create a view of the world you operate in, rather than specifically trying to figure out what your sales will be

---

THINK about it!

How certain would you be of being able to predict the following (from 0 – not very confident, to 10 – very confident)?

■ The time it gets dark tomorrow ☐
■ The value of the euro next week ☐
■. The time of the news on television next week ☐
■ How many hours you will work this weekend ☐
■ Manchester United FC beating Oxford United FC ☐

Why are you more certain of some estimates than others?

Planning for the end of the world

You're the boss, you're in charge. So it's your job to plan. But what precisely should you plan for? Everything and anything? Not possible. You need to take a view of which events are most likely to occur and how dangerous they are if they do. Some plans are clearly essential (although this does not mean everyone actually produces them!) – eg it's fairly clear that you need to plan your sales, your workforce requirements, your cashflow and your production scheduling. But what about planning for events that are unlikely but which may happen? This involves risk assessment.

Assessing risk

Risk assessment is not rocket science – all you have to do is consider which events are most likely, what the possible consequences would be and plan accordingly. Many organisations will have risk assessment committees at a senior level reporting on possible events and taking control of plans for various situations. In a similar way, the government will have plans for a sudden cold spell, floods or a nuclear attack. However, risk assessment does require management time and effort, and many managers would rather plan for the here and now than the possible, the 'maybe'. Plan properly and you will have a fallback position. You will have a crisis team organised and a plan about what to do – eg new possible suppliers to use, another manager who has the skills to stand in. The problem is that there are so many things that could happen that you need to make sure you are not spending time focusing on the wrong things. You could be fretting over the danger of a financial crisis when the real issue is a potential production problem.

Professor Mitroff, professor of business policy at the University of Southern California, categorises seven possible crises that firms may plan for. These are:
- economic changes such as strikes or collapse in profits
- 'informational' disasters such as a loss of computer records
- damage to company's reputation
- human resource incidents such as workplace violence
- natural disasters such as flooding
- the loss of key facilities
- psychopathic acts including terrorism.

The process of preparing for a possible event in advance is called 'contingency planning'. Once the event has actually happened, you are into the world of crisis management. If you've planned in advance it should be so much easier – you kick-start your plan and away you go. Without any plan you have to start from scratch, in a hurry. This puts even more pressure on you at a time you least need it.

Crisis management: Ford, Johnson & Johnson, Coca Cola

One company that faced a major crisis in 2001 was Ford. The company ran into a massive safety and public relations problems when the tyres on its off-road Explorer were found to be faulty. Mr Nasser, Ford's Chief Executive, had to take to the air in a TV advertising campaign in which he said 'I want all of our owners to know that there are two things that we never take lightly – your safety and your trust'. He pledged to replace 6.5 m tyres supplied by Bridgestone (the Japanese tyre manufacturer) after the faults were linked to more than 60 deaths.

One of the greatest examples of good crisis management occurred in 1982 when the US healthcare products group, Johnson and Johnson, had a problem with its headache tablets called Tylenol. An extortionist tried to blackmail the company by lacing capsules of the painkiller with cyanide; seven people died. While the government was still deciding what to do, and before the media had time to put the company on the defensive, Johnson and Johnson recalled all of its Tylenol products. It was not prepared to take any risks with peoples' health. The recall cost about $100 m and lost short-term sales. But Johnson and Johnson emerged with very high consumer confidence and quickly regained its leadership of the painkiller market.

Consider the way Coca Cola handled a crisis in 1999 when some of its products were found to be contaminated. Coca Cola did eventually admit that its products going into the Belgian market had been tainted in two incidents. One involved the accidental injection of 'defective' carbon dioxide gas into some cola. In the other, the outside of soft drink cans was contaminated by a fungicide used to treat wooden shipping pallets. But the admission only came after the company had spent a week assuring consumers that its products were safe. It made that claim as dozens of Belgian children were taken to hospital, complaining of stomach cramps, vomiting and dizziness after drinking Coca Cola products. Coca Cola had intended to have a targetted withdrawal. Instead, sales of nearly all Coca Cola's canned and bottled products had already been banned by the governments of Belgium and Luxembourg.

Summary points

▶ change is ongoing and firms need to do what they can to prepare for it

▶ contingency planning involves developing a plan of how to react if an unlikely event does occur

▶ risk assessment involves assessing the risk of particular events occurring; this is an important element of contingency planning

▶ crisis management involves dealing with a crisis once it has happened

You are the managing director of an airline. Identify the three critical events for which you think you should develop a contingency plan. How would you decide how much money should be allocated to developing a plan for these three events?

What makes for business success?

If only we really knew! While we can identify features which some successful organisations seem to have in common, it seems all too easy to find other firms which do things in a completely different way. In some cases success seems planned and well thought through; in other cases it seems to take the owners by surprise as much as anyone else. So is there any thing we can learn in the study of business that can help us?

It seems clear that your chances are improved if you have a good idea of who your customers are, and have thought carefully about what enables you (rather than your rivals) to attract and keep customers now and in the future. Information and empathy matter. Obsession and passion seem to help as well – obsession with quality, with getting it right, with meeting customer needs, with getting employees involved; passion for your products and for providing an excellent service. Firms now seem to recognise the importance of obsession: Odeon Cinemas is 'Fanatical about Film', whilst The Tote bookmaker is 'passionate about betting'.

It also seems that successful businesses have particular strengths that are not easy for others to imitate – whether this be its people, its culture, its brands or its technology. These can provide a competitive advantage.

Opinions on achieving success

According to Gary Hamel and CK Prahalad in their book, *Competing for the Future*[5], a competitive advantage is based on a firm's 'core competencies'. Hamel and Prahalad define these as 'the skills that enable a firm to deliver a fundamental customer benefit'. For example, Sony has been superb at miniaturisation, Swatch at design (which has been taken into producing cars), Disney at entertainment, The Carphone Warehouse at providing impartial, well-informed, useful advice. According to Hamel and Prahalad firms must look for areas where their skills match the market opportunities.

Another writer, John Kay[6], argues that a firm's success is derived from what he calls its 'distinctive capabilities'. A distinctive capability is sustainable and belongs to the firm alone (ie competitors cannot easily get hold of it). It may be achieved through:

- innovation – assuming this innovation can be protected (eg through a patent)
- its 'architecture' – this is the system of relationships within the firm or between the firm and its suppliers and customers. These relationships provide firms with the information, experience and flexibility they need to win
- its reputation – this is something others cannot easily imitate and cannot build quickly. A good reputation provides a protective shield.

To continue being successful, firms must protect or develop their competitive advantages – success is not a given. Successful firms do not stand still and rely on their advantages always being there; they push forward, developing their new strengths and finding new ways to compete or new arenas to compete in.

Continued success also requires an acceptance by management that they cannot know everything – if they wait until they do they will never act. They need to be willing to learn and be open to new ideas. They need to monitor those around them and listen actively. As Peter Senge says in his best-selling book, *The Fifth Discipline*[7]: 'The organisations that will truly excel in the future will be the organisations that discover how to tap people's commitment and capacity to learn at all levels in an organisation … In its simplest form a learning organisation is a group of people who are continually enhancing their capability to create the future'.

Characterisitics of excellent companies

In the 1990s Tom Peters and Robert Waterman wrote *In Search of Excellence*[8]. This became one of the best-selling management books of all time, selling over five million copies. They identified the characteristics of excellent companies, which:

- had a bias for action, for example the boss of Anschutz, which made a bid to take on the Millenium Dome, said 'when you take action you create the outcome'
- were close to the customer – this stresses the need to be market orientated
- had autonomy and entrepreneurship, ie individual employees were encouraged to act for themselves and use their initiative. This ties in with developments such as more democratic management and empowerment
- believed in productivity through people, ie that people provide a huge contribution to an organisation and one which is not easily imitated by competitors
- were hands-on and value-driven
- 'stuck to the knitting' (kept to their core activities)
- had a simple form and lean staff
- had simultaneous loose-tight properties (ie they were tough and set out key policies where they needed to, but otherwise encouraged initiative and independent thinking and action).

Since writing this book, Peters and Waterman have been criticised for the fact that several of the companies that featured in it have since declined in performance. In response Peters went on to write various books including *Thriving on Chaos*, stressing the turbulent world in which all firms operate and the fact that this means continued business success is extremely unpredictable. Admittedly there are still some fairly major old brands around – Kellogg, Heinz, Coca Cola and so on, but these organisations have had to work hard at it. The decline of Marks and Spencer is a warning to us all; hailed as the all-conquering retail hero in the 1990s when it achieved profits of over £1 bn, its profits fell significantly by 2001. What happened? It lost its competitive advantage. It was renowned for Quality, Service and Value (its own motto); it stopped offering this and customers naturally went elsewhere. A failure to stock the right products, an increasing failure to keep up with market trends and a conservative approach eventually caught up with it. However, the later revival of Marks and Spencer also demonstrates the ability of organisations to fight back – decline does not have to be terminal.

The importance of flexibility

Business success is not static. It is not something you achieve and then can keep forever. Witness the collapse of the multibillion dollar Enron in 2002 and the knock-on effects on its auditors Arthur Andersen. Giants one minute; humbled the next. Success has to be protected and maintained. As you watch business organisations over time, they change shape and strategies to stay one step ahead of the game. Success therefore involves flexibility and the ability to react to or anticipate change.

For a good example of flexibility just look at Timpson, a 30-year-old UK family business. This company has certainly not stood still over the years: it has always been willing to change to ensure its survival. It started off as a business selling shoes and then moved into shoe repair. Then it extended into key cutting, then engraving and then watch repair. At each stage the company has built on its strengths – namely, over 300 outlets in city centre locations, and highly motivated and empowered employees willing to learn new skills; it has seized new opportunities to move the business forward. As the present chairman John Timpson says, 'if you had told me what we would be doing 10 years ago I would never have believed you. This business is like a giraffe. If a child drew such a thing on a piece of paper you would think it was out of its mind. But when you see it running about in reality it works perfectly well'.

Integration – bringing it all together

The success of a business clearly depends on many factors coming together at the right time in the right place – which is probably why success is so difficult to predict. It involves the effective integration of the different activities within a firm. A business is made up of many different units, each with its own challenges and issues, but in order to succeed all the various aspirations and focus of these departments must be brought together. The different functional areas of the firm (marketing, HRM, production and operations) must cooperate and act in unison. And there must be the flexibility to change the ways these work and interrelate in relation to the external environment.

Firms often lose their way precisely because of a lack of coordination within the business. Marketing promises a launch date but production problems fail to produce the goods. Finance fails to raise the necessary finance of the much-needed expansion. HRM cannot attract the staff required to provide the high quality service needed to compete.

While it may be possible to identify specific aspects of particular firms which seem an important part of their success – their innovation, staff, brand values, distribution, basic recipe – in reality there must be a combination of factors for the business as a whole to work. Reading business books cannot ensure that all the factors combine at the right time, but they may inspire you to look at things in a different way and shape conditions more favourably for success.

Summary points

- ▶ success involves flexibility

- ▶ success requires a bias for action

- ▶ success depends on having a cost or benefit advantage

- ▶ sustainable success relies on being able to maintain a cost or benefit advantage rather than having a one-off success

THINK about it!

Having read this book and hopefully thought about businesses all around you, what do you think are the *three* most important factors that determine whether a business is successful?

References

1. Charles B. Handy *Understanding Organisations* 4th Edition (Penguin, 1992)
2. Kurt Lewin *Field Theory in Social Science* (Harper, 1951)
3. M. Hammer and J. Champy *Reengineering the Corporation* Revised edition (Nicholas Brealey, 2001).
4. John Kotter and Leonard Schlesinger 'Choosing Strategies for Change' *Harvard Business Review* (1979).
5. G. Hamel and C.K. Prahalad *Competing for the future* (Harvard Business School Press, 1994)
6. John Kay *Foundations of Corporate Success* (Oxford, 1995)
7. Peter Senge *The Fifth Discipline* (Random House, 1993)
8. Tom Peters and Robert Waterman *In Search of Excellence* (HarperCollins, 1995)

Suggested answers

The questions at the end of each unit are intended to get you thinking about the key issues in the book. As with most issues in business, there is no right or wrong answer, there are just different views! Below are *suggested* answers to some of the end-of-unit questions.

Business format

 **(Page 11) Identify three key factors you would need to know before deciding.**

3 key factors	Reason selected
1. Risk of being sued	Does she need limited liability? Is it worth the costs of establishing a company, eg audit costs?
2. How much has she got to lose?	Again, is limited liability actually necessary?
3. Desire for privacy	Is she willing to publish how much she earns?

Under what circumstances would you recommend her to go ahead?
If she is worried about having unlimited liability and the costs of being a company (eg audit fees) can easily be covered by the business she should form a company.

 **(Page 11) Identify three key factors Charles should take into account.**

3 key factors	Reason selected
1. How serious are the rifts?	Present position may not be sustainable if it is going to split the family – how bad are the disagreements?
2. Who has the majority votes?	Those who want to float may only have a small percentage of the votes and can be ignored.
3. What is the likely impact of bringing in outside investors?	Eg what will it do to Charles' position? Is his job likely to be threatened?

Under what circumstances would you advise Charles to go ahead?
If he feels that not doing so will split the family and if this matters to him. If he believes the flotation will not ruin the firm by changing the way it is run. If he feels they will be able to sell the shares for an appropriate price.

Shareholders

(Page 15) **Questions for the managing director of Electron plc**

Questions	Reason(s) why this is important to know
1. Projected profits of the business?	Likely to affect share price – would be useful to have some idea of expected profits. This would affect dividends and investment.
2. Likely market developments, eg new competitors, contracts up for renewal?	You may want to assess the impact of such changes on the firm's value. Obviously important to know any possible/likely market developments and possible consequences for the firm.
3. How prepared is the management for growth?	You need to be sure the firm can cope with growth, eg sufficient management expertise, effective systems for coordination and control.

Starting up is hard to do

(Page 17) **Questions for Hildegard Henshaw**

Questions	Reason(s) why this is important to know
1. What is the idea?	Need to assess viability – is it realistic? Can it be produced? Is it as wonderful as she thinks? Can the idea be protected, eg via a patent?
2. Financial projections	How is it to be marketed? What is its Unique Selling Proposition? What are the likely sales and profits?
3. Management	Who is going to manage the project? Do they have sufficient expertise and experience?

How not to do it

(Page 22) **Checklist for start-up success**

Factors to check	Reason
1. Determination	Likely to face setbacks
2. Multiskilled	Likely to have to turn your hand to many things
3. Creativity	Need to think of new solutions and novel ways of doing things
4. Obsession	Need to be focused
5. Passion	Need to be willing to give your all even when the going gets tough

Growing pains

(Page 24) **Identify three factors which would make you decide.**

Factor	Reason why important
1. Costs	You need to know what you are expected to spend and whether you can raise these funds (if you can't, forget it!)
2. Profits	What are past profits of the business? How do they compare with the investment required? What are projected profits?
3. Personal issues	Do you want to manage another shop? Could you cope with having to watch over two rather than one? Is it worth the stress?

Stages of growth

(Page 30) **Identify three factors that would determine whether or not you made an offer for the business.**

Factor	Reason why important
1. Potential profitability of the business	Whether or not it has been making a profit in the past may matter less than your view of whether you can make profits in the future. These returns need comparing with alternatives.
2. What is asking price?	Never forget the price! Something is only worth buying if the price is right. How does the price compare with the expected returns?
3. Degree of 'fit'	How will the two businesses fit together? Are there likely to be cultural problems? Can your management cope with managing the two businesses? What gains will occur with the two firms working together?

Types of strategy

(Page 47) **Do you think it is possible to be both a 'differentiated' and 'low cost' provider?**

Porter worried about firms being 'caught in the middle'. Firms could end up providing an average service at a high price. The danger of trying to achieve a "low cost" position and a "differentiated" position may be that you set out to differentiate but to cut costs you reduce the quality of your service. In fact, some firms do appear to be offering high quality, differentiated products at a relatively low price and have been successful as a result, eg Sony.

Where do strategies come from, boss?

(Page 50) **Football**

- Strategy: may play defensively so you do not lose too many matches.
- Reason for choosing the strategy: good, strong defensive players; manager dislikes risk of attacking and losing.
- Reason to abandon the existing strategy: not working! Losing game.s

How should you manage?

(Page 56) **What are the main factors that will influence your management style and why?**

Factor	Reason
1. What has worked for you in the past	If it works, why change?
2. Likely attitude of new employees	May need to make your mark and quell rebellion!
3. What you need to achieve	Rapid, unpleasant change may take an authoritarian style.

Leadership in action: Jack Welch

(Page 58) **Do you think such people are born as leaders, or can you train people to become great managers?**

There may well be certain personality traits which help people succeed as leaders, but there does not seem to be any set formula. Numerous tests and surveys have been done to isolate the key features of leadership but so far no 'magic formula' has been found. Training seems to be important, and companies can give employees the experience they need. The answer is likely to be a mixture of 'nature' and 'nurture'.

Analysing culture and culture change

(Page 65) **Managing the pub**

Obviously you need to make your mark as the new boss, and clearly there needs to be a major shake-up in terms of what is going on at the pub. Punishing someone to set an example may act as a sudden wake-up call for the others, but be careful you are not breaking any laws. You cannot dismiss someone just because you feel like it. Would it be better to make it clear that you want change and give people a chance to change their behaviour? You can then come down hard on them when you have given them a warning of what would happen if they fail to perform. Also, look at what is causing these problems – are the staff naturally lazy, or is it due to the rewards and way they have been managed before? Perhaps the managers are responsible, in which case you should look at how you manage them before making an example of them.

Market research

(Page 84) **Decide whether or not to do more research.**

- How much will research cost?
- How long will it take?
- To what extent does it matter when the book is published?
- How will the nature of the research differ from getting extra readers?
- How much risk is involved – what amount of money is invested in this project?
- How much do you trust your readers and your own instincts?

The finance department

(Page 105) **Management accounting v financial accounting.**

Obviously both matter. Management accounting will help managers decide what they are supposed to do, eg whether to go ahead with an investment and what price to charge. However, once these decisions have been taken, we do need to record what has actually happened to see whether or not the plan has worked (otherwise we won't know whether the projections of the management accounting were appropriate). Also, financial accounting is important to produce the records necessary to decide how much profit the firm has made and what assets it has; these are essential for investors.

What is profit?

(Page 108) **Identify three indicators to measure the success of the following organisations.**

Organisation	Measure 1	Measure 2	Measure 3
Sixth Form College	Exam results	Attendance	Number applying to join
Prison	Re-offending rates	Number of incidents in the prison	Number taking part in a training activity
Charity	Funds raised	Administration costs as a percentage of turnover	Number of people helped
Library	Number of books stocked	Number of subscribers	Average number of books taken out
Restaurant	Number of customers	Rating in guide books	Profits

Can you trust the figures?

 (Page 110) **Do you window-dress the accounts?**
My decision (doesn't have to be yours!): yes

Why?
- it is legal
- it gives me a breathing space to make improvements
- other firms are probably doing it so we are likely to be losing out if we don't.

Depends on:
- skill and integrity of analyst – don't want anything illegal
- my confidence that I can turn it around in the future, otherwise it may be better to face the music now.

Ratio analysis

 (Page 114) **Which of the two companies below would you invest in?**
My decision (does not have to be yours!): Company A

Why?
- highest profitability. However, the gearing is relatively high and so you would need to consider the firm's interest payments
- the acid test is fine, suggesting no major liquidity problems
- the PE ratio is low and so this may mean the share price is relatively low; may mean it can increase in the future
- ultimately depends more on expectations of the future than past figures

What is Human Resource Management?

 (Page 121) **Ageing population**

- may affect recruitment policies – need to try and attract older workers
- may affect employment policies, eg extend retirement age
- may try harder to retain staff
- may affect types of rewards offered and job design, eg greater flexibility for working hours

Motivating your staff

(Page 128) **Head Teacher of a secondary school**

- may look at duties and responsibilities and see if these can be redesigned in any way
- may look at way staff are managed
- may look at rules/regulations
- any way of reducing administrative load affecting staff
- offer individuals greater responsibility in areas they are interested in

Before deciding what to do:
- need to discuss with staff what the key issues are; the best ideas are likely to come from staff themselves – they are the ones who know what is dissatisfying them. However, they would need to realise the constraints you face
- key decision is how to consult – is this done on an individual basis or by meeting staff representatives?

Lean and mean

(Page 145) **Toyota**
My decision (does not have to be yours!): no

Reasoning: making a product is not enough, you also have to sell it! This involves promoting the product so people know about it, setting the right price and ensuring it is distributed effectively. It also depends on the competition and what they are doing and external factors such as consumers' incomes. Success depends on several factors working effectively together rather than just one factor.

Quality is cheap

(Page 153) **Crosby – What do you need to know?**

I need to know...	Because...
1. How exactly will it be used?	Need to know the purpose and what the expected outcomes are.
2. Who will be involved in the training – numbers, how selected?	Part of the process of assessing the value of the training.
3. What other demands are there on the money?	Always need to think about the opportunity costs.

Choosing projects

(Page 160) **Shoe factory – What do you need to know?**

I need to know...	Because...
1. likely market conditions	No point expanding if the demand is not there.
2. cost of expansion	Will need to know how much can be raised – is it feasible?
3. unit costs	Will the venture be profitable? What rate of return is likely?
4. the owner's views	eg What is their attitude to risk? Do they want to expand?

Project management

(Page 162) **The party**

What other information do you need from your boss?
- What is the budget?
- Who exactly will be invited – total numbers?
- Type of event required – formal/informal?
- What is he/she expecting in terms of entertainment, food etc?

Identify the key activities involved in organising such an event.
Depends on event, but you need:
- venue
- to get invitations designed, printed and sent out
- to book catering
- to organise entertainment
- organise any special displays, etc.

Identify the order in which the various activities must occur (or whether they can be undertaken at the same time as other events).
Key thing to get right first is probably the venue; obviously invites can only be done after this; also catering, entertainment, etc may depend on the venue.

Estimate the overall time to get the project completed.
Could probably be done in a matter of weeks (but depends on scale of event).

Innovation

(Page 166) **Research and development – What information do you need?**

I need to know...	Because...
1. future plans	To what extent are we relying on new product developments to generate sales?
2. availability of funds	If the money isn't there, you can't spend it!
3. what competitors are spending	Useful to have some kind of benchmark.
4. what the predicted turnover will be	Need to get some kind of absolute figure.

The Economic Environment

(Page 174) **Economic trends**

Depends on the economic trends! But the taxi firm is more likely to be more affected by the local economy than the national. In a boom we may buy more electrical goods and computers but may shop less at charity shops.

Competitive forces and Mr Porter

(Page 180) **UK food retail sector**

Entry threat:
expensive to enter and compete head on with the major firms;
easier/cheaper to set up as small local retailer

Rivalry: quite intense between major firms; although some allegations of collusion

Supplier power:
limited; major
supermarkets have
enormous buying power
over suppliers
and lots of options (ie can
change quite easily)

Buyer power:
customers have ability
to take business
elsewhere, hence
attempts by stores to
build loyalty (eg loyalty cards)

Substitute threat:
limited – we need food!

Social responsibility

(Page 185) **Should a firm be held responsible for the actions of its suppliers?**
Your decision: It depends

Reasoning: you might argue that a firm should be responsible for some elements of its suppliers' actions but not all. For example, it should make sure the product it has designed/ordered from the supplier is safe but should not be held responsible if, for example, the suppliers' managers wrongly dismiss their staff. Ultimately suppliers must be responsible for their own actions.

Social responsibility in action

(Page 189) **Is it worth being socially responsible?**
Your decision: It depends!

Reasoning: there are obviously potential benefits, including favourable customer and media reaction and more interest from some investors and employees. However, behaving socially responsibly can reduce profits, eg you may pay more than you have to to suppliers and employees. So the impact on profits depends on factors such as: how much do consumers, employees, investors really care? Also, you may need to consider each activity on a case-by-case basis – some actions may improve profits; some may reduce profits.

The question asks whether it is 'worth' being socially responsible, in which case profits may not be the key issue. Whether or not profits rise, you may feel it is the right thing to do and therefore is worth it. It depends on your priorities. There is certainly more pressure on firms nowadays to behave more responsibly.

Business and ethics

(Page 192)

- **Do you let the customer buy the blue dress?**
  Your decision: yes or no? Up to you – how honest do you want to be? how important is the sale? is it an important customer?
- **Do you tell the clients about the damp?**
  Your decision: yes or no? Again it's up to you! How honest are you!
- **Identify three key factors to decide whether or not to relocate.**

3 key factors	Reasoning
1. How great are the savings ?	Need to know exactly how much you would gain by moving.
2. How many jobs would be lost?	Need to know the consequences of your decision.
3. Do you care what happens in the area?	Your attitudes are clearly very important – do you believe in social responsibility?

- **Identify two key pieces of information you would like to have before deciding whether to accept the contract or not.**

2 key pieces of information	Reason selected
Does anyone care how the products are made?	If not, maybe it is not a big issue.
Are the allegations true?	Don't assume they are!

Globalisation

 (Page 196) **Global goods and services**

Global Goods	Global service
1. Marlboro	1. CNN
2. Sony	2. MTV
3. Coca Cola	3. American Express

Why do you think these brands have been successful? Do you think it is easier to be global with some kinds of products and services than others? Why?

The ability of a product or service to go global depends on:
- extent to which local tastes differ
- distribution – can they get to the market?
- marketing power/skill of the firm.

Do you think it has become easier or more difficult for products to succeed globally? Why?

Probably easier – technological developments mean that via the media it is easier for everyone to see what is going on around the world. New ideas, new fashion and new trends can move around the world more quickly. Also, there has been a fall in trade barriers (eg the growth of the European Union) which has opened up markets.

Planning for the end of the world

 (Page 206) **Airline**

Identify three critical events:

- terrorist attack
- plane malfunction
- passengers getting aggressive during the flight

How would you decide how much money should be allocated to developing a plan for these three events?

- Need to think about likelihood and severity of the consequences.
- Need to think about how to prevent the above occurring, or to provide a suitable reaction if they do occur. At some point, have to make a judgement about what is an acceptable level of risk. Flying a plane can never be 100% safe – need to decide on how safe you want to make it; the safer you want it the more it is likely to cost.
- Obviously some of these decisions will be taken for you – the regulatory authorities will insist on certain standards being met.

Index

Note: page numbers in **bold** refer to diagrams.